# Mum's Favourite Puddings & Desserts

# Mum's Favourite Puddings & Desserts

**Bounty**
BOOKS

Mum's Favourite Puddings & Desserts

**Publisher:** Polly Manguel
**Editorial and Design Manager:** Emma Hill/Gary Almond
**Editor:** Jane Birch
**Designer:** Chris Bell/cbdesign
**Assistant Production Manager:** Caroline Alberti

Published in 2013 by Bounty Books,
a division of Octopus Publishing Group Ltd
Endeavour House, 189 Shaftesbury Avenue,
London WC2H 8JY
www.octopusbooks.co.uk

An Hachette UK Company
www.hachette.co.uk

ISBN: 978-0-753725-74-0

Printed and bound in China

# Contents

# Introduction

Who can resist a dessert? From comforting crumbles and tempting tarts to refreshing fruit-based desserts and rich ice creams, you'll find something for everyone and every occasion in this book. And, to help you get perfect results every time, here are a few basic tips and techniques.

## PASTRY

The secret to making good pastry is to keep everything cool, use a light touch and handle the pastry as little as possible. Add just enough water to mix; too much and the pastry will be sticky and the texture will be hard when baked.

## Lining a tin with pastry

**1** Roll out the pastry on a lightly floured surface until it is a little larger than the tin. Lift the pastry over the rolling pin and drape into the tin. Press over the base and up the sides of the tin with your fingers, taking care where the sides meet the base of the tin.

**2** Trim off the excess pastry with a rolling pin or small knife a little above the top of the tin to allow for shrinkage.

## SWEET SHORTCRUST PASTRY

### Makes 470 g (15 oz)

250 g (8 oz) plain flour
pinch of salt
50 g (2 oz) caster sugar
125 g (4 oz) butter, diced
2½–3 tablespoons iced water

Put the flour, salt and sugar in a large
mixing bowl. Add the butter and rub
into the flour with your finger tips, or use
a freestanding electric mixer, until the
mixture resembles fine crumbs.

Gradually add just enough water to enable
the crumbs to be squeezed together to
form a soft, but not sticky, dough. Knead
very lightly until smooth, then roll out on a
lightly floured surface and use to line a tart
case or top a pie.

## PÂTE SUCRÉE

### Makes 375 g (12 oz)

175 g (6 oz) plain flour
40 g (1½ oz) icing sugar
100 g (3½ oz) butter, diced
2 egg yolks

Put the flour, icing sugar and butter into
a large mixing bowl and mix with your
fingertips, or use a freestanding electric
mixer, until the mixture resembles fine
crumbs.

Add the egg yolks and mix together until
you have a soft ball. Wrap in clingfilm and
chill for 15 minutes before using.

### Baking blind

This means baking the pastry case on its
own before the filling is added.

**1**  Stand the tart tin on a baking sheet,
then prick the pastry base with a fork.
**2**  Line the pastry case with a piece of
greaseproof or nonstick baking paper
large enough to cover the base and sides
of the case. Add a generous layer of baking

beans (available from cook stores and supermarkets) or use dried pasta or pulses. Bake in a preheated oven as directed in the recipe.

## Fluting

For a professional finish, flute the edges of a pie by pressing the first and second fingers onto the pie edge, then make small cuts with a knife between them to create a scalloped edge. Repeat all around the pie.

## CHOCOLATE

### Melting chocolate

To melt chocolate, break it into pieces and heat for 5 minutes or so in a heatproof bowl set over a saucepan about one-third full of gently simmering water. Make sure that the base of the bowl cannot come in contact with the water. Don't stir the chocolate until it looks melted, then stir a couple of times until it is smooth. Overstirring will ruin the texture.

### Chocolate curls

Decorative chocolate curls are easy to make using a swivel-bladed vegetable peeler. Place a bar of chocolate on a chopping board with the smooth underside uppermost. Run the vegetable peeler blade along the top of the chocolate with the handle almost touching the edge of the bar. If the curls are very small, warm the chocolate in 10-second bursts in the microwave on full power or very briefly in a warm oven. As the chocolate softens, the curls will increase in size.

## WHIPPING CREAM

Many people tend to overwhip cream. Overwhipping makes the cream take on a grainy, almost buttery, texture and spoils the finish of the dessert. The secret is to whisk the cream until it just begins to form soft swirls, as it will thicken slightly as it stands.

## MERINGUES

When making meringues the bowl needs to be both dry and completely grease-free. If you drop any yolk at all into the whites when separating the eggs, scoop it out with a piece of shell as even the tiniest amount of yolk will prevent the whites from whisking.

**1** Whisk the whites until very stiff so they will stand in moist-looking peaks. If you're not sure whether they're ready, turn the bowl upside down – if the egg whites stay put, they're ready; if they begin to slide or fall out, whisk a little more.

**3** Shape the meringues by spooning onto a baking sheet lined with nonstick baking paper and bake according to the recipe until the meringues are crisp and can easily be lifted off the paper. If they stick to the paper, they aren't ready. Return to the oven for 10–20 minutes and test again.

**2** Gradually whisk in the sugar a teaspoonful at a time. When all the sugar has been added, whisk for a few minutes more until the meringue is very thick and glossy.

# Winter Warmers

Chocolate Puddle Pudding
Cranberry Eve's Pudding
Sussex Pond Pudding
Orchard Fruit Crumble
Sticky Fig & Banana Pudding
Baked Jam Roly Poly
Rice Pudding with Toasted Nuts
Apple & Blackberry Pie
Baked Apples
Autumn Fruit Oaty Crumble
Cranberry Sponge Puddings
Hot Blackberry & Apple Trifle
Treacle Pudding
Blackberry Charlotte
Apricot & Blueberry Cobbler
Orange, Rhubarb & Ginger Slump
Semolina Cherry Pudding

# Chocolate Puddle Pudding

**Serves 4–6**
**Preparation time 15 minutes**
**Cooking time 15 minutes**

75 g (3 oz) unsalted butter,
   at room temperature
75 g (3 oz) light soft brown
   sugar
3 eggs
65 g (2½ oz) self-raising flour
3 tablespoons cocoa powder
½ teaspoon baking powder
icing sugar, to decorate

**Sauce**

2 tablespoons cocoa powder
50 g (2 oz)  light soft brown
   sugar
250 ml (8 fl oz) boiling water

Rub a little of the butter all over the base and sides of a cooking dish and stand the dish on a baking sheet. Put the butter, sugar and eggs in a large bowl and sift in the flour, cocoa powder and baking powder. Beat together with a wooden spoon until they form a smooth mixture. Spoon the pudding mixture into the dish and spread the top level.

Put the cocoa and sugar for the sauce into a small bowl and mix in a little of the measurement boiling water to make a smooth paste. Gradually mix in the rest of the water, then pour the cocoa sauce over the pudding mixture.

Bake in a preheated oven, 180°C (350°F), Gas Mark 4, for 15 minutes or until the sauce has sunk to the bottom of the dish and the pudding is well risen. Sift a little icing sugar over the pudding and serve with scoops of vanilla ice cream or a little cream.

# Cranberry Eve's Pudding

**Serves 6**
**Preparation time 25 minutes**
**Cooking time 40–50 minutes**

750 g (1½ lb) cooking apples,
    quartered, cored, peeled
    and thickly sliced
125 g (4 oz) frozen cranberries
75 g (3 oz) caster sugar
1 tablespoon water
icing sugar, for dusting

## Topping
125 g (4 oz) unsalted butter, at
    room temperature, or soft
    margarine
125 g (4 oz) caster sugar
125 g (4 oz) self-raising flour
2 eggs
grated rind of 1 small orange,
    plus 2 tablespoons of the
    juice

Put the apples and cranberries into a 1.5 litre (2½ pint), 5 cm (2 inch) deep ovenproof dish and sprinkle over the sugar and water. Cook, uncovered, in a preheated oven, 180°C (350°F), Gas Mark 4, for 10 minutes.

Put the butter, sugar, flour and eggs for the topping in a bowl, and beat together until smooth. Stir in the orange rind and juice.

Spoon the mixture over the partially cooked fruit and spread into an even layer. Return to the oven and cook for 30–40 minutes until the topping is golden and the centre springs back when pressed with a fingertip. Dust with sifted icing sugar and serve warm with custard or cream.

# Sussex Pond Pudding

Serves 6
Preparation time 40 minutes
Cooking time 2½–3 hours

225 g (8 oz) self-raising flour
pinch of salt
25 g (1 oz) caster sugar
100 g (3½ oz) shredded
    vegetable suet
grated rind of 1 lemon
7 tablespoons cold water
1 large, thin-skinned lemon
3 cloves
100 g (3½ oz) unsalted butter,
    softened
100 g (3½ oz) soft dark brown
    sugar
100 g (3½ oz) currants
    (optional)

Sieve the flour and salt into a large bowl. Stir in the sugar, suet and 1 teaspoon of the grated lemon rind. Mix with the measurement water to form a soft, but not sticky, dough. Grease a 1 litre (2 pint) pudding basin. Roll out two-thirds of the pastry and use to line the base and sides of the basin, taking care that the pastry is even. Sprinkle the remaining lemon rind onto the bottom of lined basin.

Prick the lemon all over with a skewer and press the cloves into three of the incisions. Pack the butter around the lemon and roll in the brown sugar until well coated. Put the coated lemon into the basin and pack the currants, if used, and the remaining butter and sugar around it. If the lemon is too large, slice off the end so that the pastry lid can lie flat. Roll out the remaining pastry to form the lid. Dampen the pastry edges with water and lay over the top of the basin. Seal well by pressing the pastry edges firmly together. Cover the pudding with a double thickness of buttered baking paper or foil. Make a large pleat across the top of the paper or foil and tie down the edges around the basin securely using a long piece of string.

Place the pudding in a large pan of simmering water, ensuring that the water comes halfway up the sides of the basin. Cover with a tight-fitting lid and steam for 2½–3 hours, or until the suet crust is set. Top up the water as necessary.

Remove the paper or foil and allow the pudding to stand for a few minutes before inverting it onto a warmed serving plate. When the pudding is cut, the reason for its name becomes apparent, as a lemony pond of sauce flows out.

# Orchard Fruit Crumble

**Serves 6**
**Preparation time 20 minutes**
**Cooking time 30–35 minutes**

2 dessert apples
2 ripe pears
400 g (13 oz) red plums,
   quartered and pitted
2 tablespoons water
75 g (3 oz) caster sugar
100 g (3½ oz) plain flour
50 g (2 oz) unsalted butter,
   diced
50 g (2 oz) desiccated
   coconut
50 g (2 oz) milk chocolate
   chips

Peel, core and quarter the apples and pears. Slice the quarters and add the slices to a 1.2 litre (2 pint) pie dish. Add the plums and the measurement water, then sprinkle with 25 g (1 oz) of the sugar. Cover the dish with foil and bake in a preheated oven, 180°C (350°F), Gas Mark 4, for 10 minutes.

Put the remaining sugar in a bowl with the flour, add the butter and rub in with your fingertips or an electric mixer until the mixture resembles fine breadcrumbs. Stir in the coconut and chocolate chips.

Remove the foil from the fruit and spoon the crumble over the top. Bake for 20–25 minutes until the crumble topping is golden brown and the fruit is tender. Serve warm with custard or cream.

# Sticky Fig & Banana Pudding

Serves 6
Preparation time 10 minutes
Cooking time 20 minutes

125 g (4 oz) margarine or
  butter, softened
125 g (4 oz) soft brown sugar
1 teaspoon ground ginger
2 eggs
125 g (4 oz) plain flour
3 figs, quartered
1 large banana, cut into
  chunks
2 tablespoons maple syrup

Beat the margarine or butter and sugar until smooth and creamy. Add the ginger, eggs and flour and beat again until a smooth mixture is formed. Lightly grease a 23 cm (9 inch) square tin or ovenproof dish, then spoon in the mixture and level with the back of a spoon.

Toss the figs and banana with the maple syrup and arrange over the top of the pudding, pressing the fruit into the pudding in places. Bake in a preheated oven, 180°C (350°F), Gas Mark 4, for 20 minutes until the pudding is well risen and golden and the fruit is soft. Serve with ice cream or custard.

# Baked Jam Roly Poly

Serves 6
**Preparation time 30 minutes**
**Cooking time 30 minutes**

175 g (6 oz) self-raising flour
75 g (3 oz) shredded
   vegetable suet
½ teaspoon ground cinnamon
6 tablespoons cold water
5 tablespoons raspberry jam
milk, to glaze

Put the flour, suet and cinnamon into a large mixing bowl. Add the measurement water and mix to a soft dough.

Roll out the pastry to a 20 cm (8 inch) square. Lightly brush the edges with milk. Spread the jam evenly over the square, leaving a 2.5 cm (1 inch) edge all round. Starting from the furthermost edge, carefully begin to roll the pastry towards you, swiss-roll fashion. When the pudding is completely rolled, press down the edges well to secure the jam. Brush with a little milk to glaze.

Put the pudding onto a large baking sheet and bake in a preheated oven, 200°C (400°F), Gas Mark 6, for 30 minutes, or until the pastry is golden brown. Serve hot with custard or ice cream.

# Rice Pudding with Toasted Nuts

Serves 4
Preparation time 5 minutes
Cooking time 35–30 minutes

125 g (4 oz) brown pudding
    rice
750 ml (1¼ pints) milk
2 cardamom pods, lightly
    crushed
finely grated rind of ½ lemon
25 g (1 oz) soft dark brown
    sugar, plus extra to serve
    (optional)
1 vanilla pod, split in half
    lengthways
100 g (3½ oz) mixed blanched
    nuts, such as Brazil nuts,
    hazelnuts and shelled
    pistachio nuts

Put the rice in a heavy-based saucepan with the milk, cardamom, lemon rind and sugar. Scrape in the seeds from the vanilla pod and place over a medium heat. Bring to the boil, then reduce the heat, partially cover and simmer very gently, stirring regularly, for 25–30 minutes, or until the rice is tender and creamy, adding more milk if necessary.

Meanwhile, place the nuts in a small freezer bag and tap lightly with a rolling pin until they are crushed but not ground. Tip into a nonstick frying pan and dry-fry over a low heat for 5–6 minutes, stirring continuously, until golden. Tip on to a plate and leave to cool.

Spoon the rice pudding into deep bowls and sprinkle over a little extra brown sugar, if liked. Scatter over the toasted nuts and serve immediately.

# Apple & Blackberry Pie

Serves 4
Preparation time 20 minutes,
  plus chilling
Cooking time 35–40 minutes

150 g (5 oz) wholemeal flour
75 g (3 oz) plain flour
125g (4 oz) chilled butter
1 tablespoon caster sugar
pinch of salt
3 dessert apples, peeled,
  cored and sliced
1 teaspoon lemon juice
1 teaspoon almond extract
1–2 tablespoons soft dark
  brown sugar, to taste
  (optional)
200 g (7 oz) fresh or frozen
  blackberries
2 tablespoons toasted,
  chopped almonds
  (optional)

Place the flours in a large bowl, add the butter and rub in with the fingertips until the mixture resembles fine breadcrumbs. Stir in the caster sugar and salt. Mix in 3½–4½ tablespoons cold water, adding enough water to form a dough, and knead lightly until smooth. Divide into 2 balls, one slightly larger than the other. Wrap each in clingfilm and chill for 30 minutes.

Put the apples, lemon juice, almond extract and brown sugar in a bowl and toss to coat. Mix in the blackberries and set aside.

Roll out the larger ball of pastry on a lightly floured surface to fit a 23 cm (9 inch) nonstick pie tin. Press the pastry into the tin to come up the sides, moistening the edges with a little cold water. Roll out the smaller ball to fit as a lid. Spoon the fruit evenly over the pastry shell, then scatter over the almonds, if using. Top with the pastry lid, pressing down the dampened edges to seal. Trim away the excess pastry with a sharp knife.

Cut 3 small incisions in the top of the pie and place in a preheated oven, 180°C (350 °F), Gas Mark 4, for 35–40 minutes or until crisp and golden. Leave to rest for 5–10 minutes, then serve with custard or cream.

# Baked Apples

Serves 4
Preparation time 10 minutes
Cooking time 50 minutes–
   1 hour

4 large cooking apples
50 g (2 oz) dates, stoned and
   chopped
25 g (1 oz) raisins
25 g (1 oz) soft brown sugar
½ teaspoon ground cinnamon
4 tablespoons cider

Remove the cores from the apples. Make a shallow cut around the middle of each one.

Mix together the dates, raisins, sugar and cinnamon and use to fill the apple cavities, pressing down firmly.

Place in an ovenproof dish and add the cider. Bake in a preheated oven, 180°C (350°F), Gas Mark 4, for 50 minutes–1 hour, until soft. Serve hot with cream or custard.

# Autumn Fruit Oaty Crumble

**Serves 4**
**Preparation time 15 minutes**
**Cooking time 40–45 minutes**

1 dessert apple, peeled,
  cored and sliced
25 g (1 oz) ready-to-eat dried
  apples, chopped (optional)
400 g (13 oz) can pear halves
  in juice, drained with
  4 tablespoons juice
  reserved, roughly chopped
200 g (7 oz) ripe plums, halved,
  stoned and quartered
25 g (1 oz) raisins or golden
  raisins

**Topping**
75 g (3 oz) wholemeal flour
50 g (2 oz) rolled oats
25 g (1 oz) bran
pinch of salt
50 g (2 oz) pecan nuts,
  chopped
2 tablespoons soft dark
  brown sugar
¾ teaspoon mixed spice
75 g (3 oz) butter, melted

Put all of the prepared fruit and raisins into a shallow, rectangular ovenproof dish, approximately 28 x 20 cm (11 x 8 inches). Drizzle over the reserved pear juice.

Mix together the dry topping ingredients in a large bowl. Pour over the melted butter and combine until the mixture resembles large breadcrumbs. Sprinkle over the fruit and press down firmly.

Place in a preheated oven, 180°C (350°F), Gas Mark 4, for 40–45 minutes or until golden and crisp. Serve warm with Greek yogurt, custard or cream.

# Cranberry Sponge Puddings

Serves 4
Preparation time 10 minutes
Cooking time 25 minutes

finely grated rind and juice of
  1 orange
150 g (5 oz) fresh or frozen
  cranberries
100 g (3½ oz) caster sugar
2 tablespoons raspberry jam
100 g (3½ oz) butter, softened
100 g (3½ oz) self-raising flour
2 eggs

Put the orange juice into a saucepan with the cranberries and 1 tablespoon of the sugar and cook over a moderate heat for 5 minutes until the cranberries are just softened. Use a slotted spoon to drain and spoon half the cranberries into 4 individual 200 ml (7 fl oz) metal pudding moulds.

Add the jam to the remaining cranberries and cook for 1 minute until melted. Set the sauce aside.

Put the remaining sugar, butter, flour, eggs and orange rind into a bowl or food processor and beat until smooth. Spoon the sponge mixture into the moulds and level the surface. Cover loosely with pieces of oiled foil.

Cook the puddings in the top of a steamer or in a preheated oven, 180°C (350°F), Gas Mark 4, for 20 minutes until well risen. Loosen the edges with a round-bladed knife and turn out on to plates. Top with the cranberry sauce and serve with custard.

# Hot Blackberry & Apple Trifle

Serves 4
Preparation time 20 minutes,
  plus cooling
Cooking time 20–25 minutes

150 g (5 oz) fresh or frozen
  blackberries
2 dessert apples, cored,
  peeled and sliced
1 tablespoon water
50 g (2 oz) caster sugar
4 trifle sponges
3 tablespoons dry or sweet
  sherry
425 g (14 oz) can or carton
  custard

### Meringue
3 egg whites
75 g (3 oz) caster sugar

Put the blackberries, apples, measurement water and sugar in a saucepan, then cover and simmer for 5 minutes or until the fruit has softened. Leave the mixture to cool slightly.

Break the trifle sponges into chunks and arrange in an even layer in the base of a 1.2 litre (2 pint) ovenproof pie or soufflé dish and drizzle with the sherry. Spoon the poached fruit and syrup over the top, then cover with custard.

Whisk the egg whites in a large, dry bowl until stiffly peaking, then gradually whisk in the sugar, a teaspoonful at a time, until the meringue is stiff and glossy (see page 9). Spoon over the custard and swirl the top with the back of a spoon.

Bake in a preheated oven, 180°C (350°F), Gas Mark 4, for 15–20 minutes until heated through and the meringue is golden. Serve immediately.

# Treacle Pudding

Serves 4
Preparation time 25 minutes
Cooking time 1½–2 hours

125 g (4 oz) unsalted butter
125 g (4 oz) caster sugar
2 large eggs
125 g (4 oz) self-raising flour,
    sifted
4 tablespoons gold syrup

## Sauce
4 tablespoons golden syrup
1 tablespoon water

Put the butter and sugar in a large mixing bowl and cream together until light and fluffy. Beat in the eggs, one at a time, adding a little of the flour with the second egg. Fold in the remaining flour.

Grease a 900 ml (1½ pint) pudding bowl and spoon in the syrup, then put the sponge mixture on top. Cover the pudding with a double thickness of buttered baking paper or foil. Make a large pleat across the top of the paper or foil and tie down the edges around the bowl securely using a long piece of string.

Place the pudding into a large saucepan of simmering water, ensuring that the water comes halfway up the sides of the basin. Cover with a tight-fitting lid and steam for 1½–2 hours. Top up the water as necessary.

Remove the paper or foil from the basin and allow the pudding to stand for a few minutes while you make the sauce.

To make the sauce, heat the syrup and water in a small saucepan. Turn the pudding out onto a warmed serving dish and pour the hot sauce over before serving with custard or cream.

# Blackberry Charlotte

✦❧❦❧✦

Serves 4
Preparation time 10 minutes
Cooking time 20–25 minutes

500 g (1 lb) blackberries
150 g (5 oz) caster sugar
1 teaspoon vanilla extract
8 small, thin slices of white
   bread
25 g (1 oz) unsalted butter,
   softened

Place the blackberries in an ovenproof dish, then gently stir in the sugar and vanilla extract.

Cut the crusts from the bread, spread both sides with the butter and cut in half to form triangles. Arrange over the blackberries, overlapping slightly in 2 rows.

Place in a preheated oven, 190°C (375°F), Gas Mark 5, for 20–25 minutes or until the bread is golden and crisp and the fruit bubbling. Serve with custard.

# Apricot & Blueberry Cobbler

Serves 4
Preparation time 10 minutes
Cooking time 20 minutes

12 ripe apricots, halved
   and stoned
150 g (5 oz) blueberries
2 tablespoons light
   muscovado sugar
175 g (6 oz) self-raising flour,
   plus extra for dusting
50 g (2 oz) unsalted butter,
   diced
50 g (2 oz) caster sugar
125 ml (4 fl oz) buttermilk
milk, for brushing

Place the apricots and blueberries in a 750 ml (1¼ pint) ovenproof dish and sprinkle over the muscovado sugar.

Place the flour in a bowl, add the butter and rub in with the fingertips until the mixture resembles fine breadcrumbs. Stir in the caster sugar, then add the buttermilk a little at a time, to form a slightly sticky, soft dough.

Turn the dough out on to a lightly floured surface and pat out until it is 1 cm (½ inch) thick. Cut out 8 rounds using a 6 cm (2½ inch) cutter.

Arrange over the top of the fruit and brush with a little milk. Place in a preheated oven, 180°C (350°F), Gas Mark 4, for 20 minutes or until the scones are golden and the fruit is bubbling. Serve immediately.

# Orange, Rhubarb & Ginger Slump

Serves 6
Preparation time 10 minutes
Cooking time 20 minutes

750 g (1½ lb) rhubarb,
    chopped into 1.5 cm
    (¾ inch) pieces
½ teaspoon ground ginger
50 g (2 oz) golden caster
    sugar
grated rind and juice of
    1 orange
4 tablespoons mascarpone
    cheese
175 g (6 oz) self-raising flour,
    sifted
50 g (2 oz) unsalted butter,
    diced
grated rind of ½ lemon
6 tablespoons milk

Put the rhubarb, ginger, half the sugar and orange rind and juice into a medium saucepan. Bring to the boil and simmer gently for 5–6 minutes until the rhubarb is just tender. Transfer to an ovenproof dish and spoon over dollops of mascarpone.

Place the flour in a bowl. Add the butter and rub with the fingertips until the mixture resembles fine breadcrumbs. Quickly stir through the remaining sugar, the lemon rind and milk until combined. Place spoonfuls of the mixture over the rhubarb and mascarpone.

Cook in a preheated oven, 200°C (400°F), Gas Mark 6, for 12–15 minutes until golden and bubbling. Serve with custard or cream.

# Semolina Cherry Pudding

**Serves 4**
**Preparation time 10 minutes**
**Cooking time 20 minutes**

25 g (1 oz) semolina
600 ml (1 pint) milk
2 tablespoons granulated
  sugar
1 egg yolk, beaten
2–3 drops almond extract
15 g (½ oz) flaked almonds
  (optional)

**Cherry sauce**
425 g (14 oz) can pitted black
  cherries
2 teaspoons arrowroot
1 tablespoon caster sugar

Put the semolina is a jug or small bowl and blend with a little of the milk. Put the remaining milk into a saucepan and heat until almost boiling. Pour the heated milk onto the semolina, stir well and return to the saucepan. Stir in the granulated sugar and bring to the boil. Simmer gently for 10–15 minutes, or until the mixture has thickened, stirring occasionally.

Remove from the heat and stir in the beaten egg, almond extract and flaked almonds, if using.

While the semolina is cooking, prepare the cherry sauce. In a small saucepan blend the can of cherries with the arrowroot and caster sugar. Bring the sauce to the boil, stirring continuously.

Spoon the semolina into individual serving dishes and top with the cherry sauce.

# Chilled to Perfection

Blackcurrant & Mint Soufflé
Gooseberry Fool with Lemon Thins
Apple & Blackberry Fool
Coffee & Walnut Cream
Rich Chocolate Mousse
Vanilla Crème Brûlée
Pyramid Slices
Mint Choc Chip Cheesecake
Lemon Creams with Raspberries
Summer Pudding
Cheat's Lemon Dainties
Strawberry Jellies
Apricot Ambrosia
Crème Caramel
Lemony Cheesecake
White Choc & Strawberry Cheesecake
Diplomatico

# Blackcurrant & Mint Soufflé

Serves 6
Preparation time 40 minutes,
   plus chilling
Cooking time 18–20 minutes

250 g (8 oz) blackcurrants,
   defrosted if frozen
6 tablespoons water
4 teaspoons powdered
   gelatine
4 eggs, separated
200 g (7 oz) caster sugar
250 ml (8 fl oz) double cream
5 tablespoons finely chopped
   fresh mint
icing sugar, for dusting

Wrap a double thickness strip of nonstick baking paper around a 13 cm (5½ inch) diameter x 6 cm (2½ inch) deep soufflé dish so the paper stands 6 cm (2½ inches) above the top. Secure with string. Put the blackcurrants and 2 tablespoons of the measurement water in a saucepan, cover and cook gently for 5 minutes until softened. Blend until smooth, then press through a sieve.

Put the remaining water in a small heatproof bowl and sprinkle over the gelatine, making sure all the powder is absorbed. Set aside for 5 minutes, then stand the bowl in a pan half-filled with boiling water and simmer for 3–4 minutes, stirring occasionally, until the gelatine dissolves to a clear liquid.

Put the yolks and sugar in a large heatproof bowl and place over a pan of simmering water so the bowl's base is not touching the water. Whisk for 10 minutes or until the eggs are very thick and pale, and leave a trail when lifted above the mixture. Remove from the heat and continue whisking until cool. Fold in the dissolved gelatine in a thin, steady stream, then fold in the purée.

Whip the cream softly, then fold into the soufflé mix with the mint. Whisk the whites into stiff, moist-looking peaks. Fold a large spoonful into the soufflé mixture to loosen it, then gently fold in the remaining whites. Pour the mixture into the soufflé dish so that it stands above the rim of the dish. Chill for 4 hours or until set. Remove the string and paper. Arrange strips of nonstick baking paper over the soufflé top so some overlap, then dust with sifted icing sugar. Lift off the strips and serve immediately or the sugar will dissolve.

# Gooseberry Fool with Lemon Thins

Serves 6
Preparation time 30 minutes,
  plus chilling
Cooking time 20–25 minutes

500 g (1 lb) gooseberries,
  topped and tailed
75 g (3 oz) caster sugar
2 tablespoons concentrated
  elderflower cordial
2 tablespoons water
150 ml (¼ pint) double cream
135 g (4½ oz) can or carton
  custard

**Lemon thins**
50 g (2 oz) unsalted butter
50 g (2 oz) caster sugar
50 g (2 oz) golden syrup
grated rind 1 lemon, plus
  1 tablespoon of the juice
125 g (4 oz) plain flour
½ teaspoon bicarbonate
  of soda
icing sugar, for dusting

Cook the gooseberries with the sugar, cordial and measurement water in a covered saucepan for 10 minutes until soft. Purée the gooseberries and their cooking juices in a liquidizer or food processor until smooth, or rub through a sieve. Leave to cool.

Whip the cream until it forms soft swirls, then fold in the custard and gooseberry purée. Spoon into small glasses and chill.

Heat the butter, sugar, syrup and lemon rind and juice for the biscuits in a small saucepan until the butter has melted and sugar dissolved. Stir in the flour and bicarbonate of soda and mix until smooth.

Drop teaspoons of the mixture on to 2 greased baking sheets, well spaced apart, then bake in a preheated oven, 180°C (350°F), Gas Mark 4, for 10–12 minutes until browning around the edges. Cool for 10 minutes, then loosen and transfer to a wire rack. Dust with sifted icing sugar and serve with the fool.

# Apple & Blackberry Fool

Serves 6
Preparation time 10 minutes,
  plus chilling
Cooking time 15 minutes

500 g (1 lb) cooking apples,
  peeled, cored and sliced
250 g (8 oz) fresh or frozen
  blackberries, thawed if frozen
50 g (2 oz) soft brown sugar
300 ml (½ pint) double cream,
  whipped

Place the apples, blackberries and sugar in a heavy-based saucepan. Cover and simmer gently for 15 minutes, until soft. Remove from the heat and allow to cool, then purée in a liquidizer or food processor. Sieve to remove the pips.

Fold the cream into the purée, spoon into individual dishes and chill.

# Coffee & Walnut Cream

Serves 4
Preparation time 5 minutes,
  plus chilling
Cooking time 5 minutes

12 marshmallows
120 ml (4 oz) strong black
  coffee
300 ml (½ pint) double cream
50 g (2 oz) walnut pieces,
  chopped

Place the marshmallows in a small saucepan with the coffee and heat gently, stirring, until dissolved. Remove from the heat and allow to cool.

Whip the cream until it stands in soft peaks, then carefully fold into the coffee mixture with all but 2 teaspoons of the walnuts.

Spoon into individual dishes, sprinkle with remaining walnuts and chill.

# Rich Chocolate Mousse

**Serves 4**
**Preparation time 5 minutes,**
**    plus chilling**
**Cooking time 3–4 minutes**

175 g (6 oz) plain dark
    chocolate, broken into
    pieces
100 ml (3 fl oz) double cream
3 eggs, separated
cocoa powder, for dusting

Put the chocolate and cream in a heatproof bowl set over a saucepan of gently simmering water (see page 8) and stir until the chocolate has melted. Leave to cool for 5 minutes, then beat in the egg yolks one at a time.

Whisk the egg whites in a separate clean bowl until stiff, then lightly fold into the chocolate mixture until combined. Spoon the mousse into 4 dessert glasses or cups and chill for 2 hours. Dust with cocoa powder before serving.

# Vanilla Crème Brûlée

Serves 6
Preparation time 20 minutes,
  plus standing and chilling
Cooking time 25–30 minutes

1 vanilla pod
600 ml (1 pint) double cream
8 egg yolks
65 g (2½ oz) caster sugar
3 tablespoons icing sugar

Slit the vanilla pod lengthways and place it in a saucepan. Pour the cream into the pan, then bring almost to the boil. Take off the heat and allow to stand for 15 minutes. Lift the pod out of the cream and, holding it against the side of the saucepan, scrape the black seeds into the cream. Discard the rest of the pod.

Use a fork to mix together the egg yolks and caster sugar in a bowl. Reheat the cream, then gradually mix it into the eggs and sugar. Strain the mixture back into the saucepan.

Place 6 ovenproof ramekins in a roasting tin, then divide the custard between them. Pour warm water around the dishes to come halfway up the sides, then bake in a preheated oven, 180°C (350°F), Gas Mark 4, for 20–25 minutes until the custard is just set with a slight softness at the centre.

Leave the dishes to cool in the water, then lift them out and chill in the refrigerator for 3–4 hours. About 25 minutes before serving, sprinkle with the icing sugar and caramelize using a blowtorch (or under a hot grill), then leave at room temperature.

# Pyramid Slices

Serves 10
Preparation time 20 minutes, plus chilling
Cooking time 10 minutes

300 g (10 oz) milk chocolate, broken into pieces
100 ml (3½ fl oz) evaporated milk
175 g (6 oz) digestive biscuits, broken into small pieces
125 g (4 oz) stoned dates, prunes or dried apricots, roughly chopped
100 g (3½ oz) mixed nuts, chopped
50 g (2 oz) plain dark chocolate

Heat the milk chocolate gently in a heavy-based pan with the evaporated milk, stirring frequently, until the chocolate has melted. Remove from the heat and transfer to a bowl. Leave until cool, but not set. Stir in the biscuits, dried fruit and nuts.

Grease the base and 3 sides of a deep 18 cm (7 inch) square cake tin and line with clingfilm. Prop up one side of the tin so that it sits at an angle of 45 degrees and the unlined side of the tin is uppermost. Spoon in the cake mixture and level the surface. Leave until firm, then transfer to the refrigerator to set completely. Remove the cake from the tin and peel away the film.

Melt the plain dark chocolate (see page 8). Using a teaspoon, drizzle lines of melted chocolate over the cake. Leave to set again, then serve thinly sliced.

# Mint Choc Chip Cheesecake

**Serves 4–6**
**Preparation time 12 minutes,**
  **plus chilling**

200 g (7 oz) chocolate biscuits
100 g (3½ oz) mint-flavoured
  dark chocolate, chopped
50 g (2 oz) butter, melted
200 g (7 oz) cream cheese
200 g (7 oz) mascarpone
  cheese
50 g (2 oz) caster sugar
1 tablespoon crème de
  menthe or peppermint
  extract
2 drops green food colouring
50 g (2 oz) plain dark
  chocolate chips

Put the biscuits and chocolate in a food processor or blender and process to make fine crumbs. Mix with the melted butter and press the mixture gently over the base of a 20 cm (8 inch), round, springform cake tin. Place in the freezer to set while making the cream cheese mixture.

Beat together the cream cheese, mascarpone, sugar, mint liqueur or extract and food colouring in a large bowl. Stir in 40 g (1½ oz) of the chocolate chips and spoon the mixture over the biscuit base, smoothing with the back of a spoon.

Place in the refrigerator to chill for about 1 hour.

Loosen the edge with a knife, then remove the cheesecake from the tin carefully. Scatter over the remaining chocolate chips, roughly chopped.

# Lemon Creams with Raspberries

Serves 4
Preparation time 5 minutes,
  plus chilling
Cooking time 5 minutes

400 ml (14 fl oz) double cream
100 g (3½ oz) caster sugar
100 ml (3½ fl oz) lemon juice
150 g (5 oz) fresh raspberries
2 tablespoons icing sugar

Heat the cream and caster sugar together in a saucepan until the sugar has dissolved. Bring to the boil, then reduce the heat and simmer for 3 minutes.

Remove the pan from the heat, add the lemon juice and immediately pour into 4 x 150 ml (¼ pint) ramekins. Set aside to cool completely, then chill overnight in the refrigerator.

Combine the raspberries and icing sugar in a bowl and mash lightly. Leave to stand for 30 minutes until really juicy. Spoon the raspberry mixture on to the lemon creams and serve.

# Summer Pudding

Serves 8
Preparation time 15 minutes,
 plus chilling
Cooking time 10–15 minutes

500 g (1 lb) fresh or frozen
 mixed redcurrants,
 blackcurrants and
 blackberries, thawed
 if frozen
125 g (4 oz) caster sugar
250 g (8 oz) fresh or frozen
 raspberries, thawed if
 frozen
8 slices white bread, crusts
 removed

Place the currants, blackberries and sugar in a heavy-based saucepan. Cook gently, stirring occasionally, for 10–15 minutes until tender. Add the raspberries, remove from the heat and leave to cool. Strain the fruit, reserving the juice.

Cut 3 rounds of bread the same diameter as a 900 ml (1½ pint) pudding basin. Shape the remaining bread to fit around the sides of the basin. Soak all the bread in the reserved juice.

Line the base of the basin with one of the rounds of bread, then arrange shaped bread around the sides. Pour in half the fruit and place another round of bread on top. Cover with the remaining fruit, then top with the remaining bread round.

Cover with a saucer small enough to fit inside the basin and put a 500 g (1 lb) weight on top. Chill in the refrigerator overnight.

Turn out onto a serving plate and pour over any remaining fruit juice. Serve with cream.

# Cheat's Lemon Dainties

**Serves 9**
**Preparation time 25 minutes, plus chilling**

8 trifle sponges, sliced in half horizontally to give shallower pieces
100 g (3½ oz) butter, softened
100 g (3½ oz) caster sugar
grated rind of 2 lemons
2 eggs, separated
150 ml (¼ pint) double cream
juice of 1 lemon

**To serve**
125 g (4 oz) fresh raspberries
100 g (3½ oz) fresh blueberries
mint leaves
4 tablespoons icing sugar, sifted

Arrange half of the trifle sponges in a single layer in the base of a 20 cm (8 inch) square shallow cake tin lined with clingfilm.

Beat together the butter, sugar and lemon rind until pale and creamy. Gradually beat in the egg yolks.

Whisk the egg whites in a large clean bowl with a hand-held electric whisk until stiff, then whip the cream in a separate bowl. Fold the whipped cream and the egg whites into the creamed mixture. Gradually fold in half the lemon juice.

Drizzle a little of the remaining lemon juice over the trifle sponges. Spoon the cream mixture on top and gently spread the surface level. Cover with a second layer of sponge slices, press them gently into the cream mixture and drizzle with the remaining lemon juice. Cover with an extra piece of clingfilm and chill for 4 hours or overnight.

Remove the top layer of clingfilm, invert the cake on to a board and peel off the remaining clingfilm. Cut into squares, decorate with berries and mint leaves and serve dusted with the sifted icing sugar.

# Strawberry Jellies

Serves 6
Preparation time 10 minutes,
plus standing and chilling
Cooking time 5 minutes

450 g (14½ oz) strawberries,
hulled
100 g (3½ oz) caster sugar
500 ml (17 fl oz) white grape
juice
2 sachets of powdered
gelatine or 6 gelatine leaves
75 ml (3 fl oz) crème de cassis
(optional)

Roughly chop three-quarters of the strawberries and put
them in a food processor or blender with 300 ml (½ pint)
boiling water and the sugar. Blend until smooth, then pour
the mixture into a sieve set over a bowl and stir to allow the
liquid to drip through.

Pour 200 ml (7 fl oz) of the grape juice into a heatproof
bowl, sprinkle over the gelatine and allow to stand for
10 minutes. Place the bowl over a saucepan of simmering
water and stir until the gelatine has dissolved. Leave to cool,
then stir in the cassis (if used), strawberry liquid and the
remaining grape juice. Arrange the remaining strawberries
in 6 large wine glasses, pour over the liquid and chill until
the jelly has set.

# Apricot Ambrosia

**Serves 4**
**Preparation time 10 minutes,
  plus chilling**

411 g (13½ oz) can apricot
  halves, drained
1 tablespoon honey
50 g (2 oz) ratafias
150 ml (¼ pint) double cream,
  whipped
1 tablespoon flaked almonds,
  toasted

Place the apricots and honey in a liquidizer or food
processor and process until smooth.

Break the ratafias into bite-size pieces and fold into the
whipped cream with the apricot purée.

Spoon into 4 individual serving dishes and chill. Sprinkle
with the flaked almonds just before serving.

# Crème Caramel

Serves 4
Preparation time 20 minutes,
  plus cooling
Cooking time 1 hour
  40 minutes

75 g (3 oz) granulated sugar
3 tablespoons water
3 eggs
25 g (1 oz) caster sugar
450 ml (¾ pint) milk
½ teaspoon vanilla extract

Put the granulated sugar and measurement water in a heavy-bottomed saucepan. Heat gently, stirring, until dissolved, then cook to a rich caramel without stirring. Remove the pan from the heat, carefully add 1 teaspoon of boiling water (the caramel may spit a bit when you do this) and pour into a 900 ml (1½ pint) soufflé dish or mould. Set aside to cool and set.

Beat the eggs and caster sugar together in a large bowl. Place the milk in a saucepan and heat almost to boiling point and pour onto the egg mixture. Add the vanilla extract and mix well.

Strain into the dish or mould over the now set caramel. Place in a roasting dish containing 2.5 cm (1 inch) water. Bake in a preheated oven, 140°C (275°F), Gas Mark 1, for 1½ hours until set. Remove from the oven and cool, then invert onto a serving dish.

# Lemony Cheesecake

Serves 6
**Preparation time 10 minutes, plus chilling**

125 g (4 oz) digestive or
    ginger biscuits, crushed
50 g (2 oz) butter, melted
250 g (8 oz) mascarpone
    cheese
grated rind and juice of
    2 lemons
150 ml (¼ pint) double cream
100 g (3½ oz) icing sugar,
    sifted

**To decorate**
blueberries and raspberries
lemon rind curls

Mix together the crushed biscuits and melted butter in a bowl, then press into the base and up the side of a 20 cm (8 inch) fluted loose-bottomed flan tin. Chill until firm.

Beat together the mascarpone, lemon rind and juice, double cream and icing sugar in a large bowl until thick, then spoon over the biscuit base. Chill for at least 30 minutes until firm.

Decorate with blueberries, raspberries and lemon rind curls, when ready to serve.

# White Choc & Strawberry Cheesecake

**Serves 6–8**
**Preparation time 30 minutes,**
   **plus chilling**

150 g (5 oz) digestive biscuits,
   crushed
75 g (3 oz) unsalted butter,
   melted
200 g (7 oz) white chocolate
   (30% cocoa solids), broken
   into small pieces
500 g (1 lb) mascarpone
   cheese
25 g (1 oz) icing sugar, sifted
200 g (7 oz) strawberries,
hulled and sliced
grated white chocolate,
   to decorate

Stir the crushed biscuits into the melted butter and press into the base of a 20 cm (8 inch) loose-bottomed round cake tin. Chill while you make the filling.

Melt the chocolate in a heatproof bowl set over a pan of gently simmering water (sce page 8), stirring occasionally.

Place the mascarpone in a bowl and whisk in the icing sugar until smooth. Whisk in the chocolate, then spread the mixture over the cheesecake base.

Chill for 15 minutes, then arrange the strawberries over the top and decorate with the grated chocolate. Serve immediately or chill until ready to serve.

# Diplomatico

Serves 8
Preparation time 25 minutes,
  plus chilling

200 g (7 oz) plain dark
  chocolate, broken into
  pieces
300 ml (½ pint) double cream
3 tablespoons icing sugar
4 tablespoons brandy or
  coffee liqueur
100 ml (3½ fl oz) strong black
  coffee, cooled
30 sponge finger biscuits

**To decorate**
150 ml (¼ pint) double cream
cocoa powder, sifted

Melt the chocolate in a heatproof bowl set over a saucepan of gently simmering water (see page 8). Meanwhile, line a 1 kg (2 lb) loaf tin with clingfilm so that the base and sides are covered.

Whip the cream until softly peaking. Fold in the icing sugar then the melted chocolate. Spoon a thin layer into the base of the lined tin.

Mix the brandy or coffee liqueur and cooled coffee in a shallow dish. Dip the sponge finger biscuits, one at a time, into the mixture to moisten then arrange in a single layer on top of the chocolate cream in the tin. Cover with half the remaining cream, then a second layer of dipped biscuits. Repeat the layers until all the cream and biscuits have been used.

Chill for 4 hours or overnight if preferred. To serve, loosen the edges and invert on to a serving plate. Peel off the clingfilm. Whip the double cream and spoon over the top, then dust with cocoa powder. Cut into thick slices to serve. Refrigerate for up to 2 days.

# Nice Ices

Chocolate Ice Cream
Old-fashioned Vanilla Ice Cream
Brown Bread Ice Cream
Cherry Almond Ice Cream
Neapolitan Whirl Ice Cream
Rum & Raisin Ice Cream
Lavender Honey Ice Cream
Fresh Fruit Lollies
Strawberry Ice Cream
Summer Berry Sorbet
Lemon Sorbet
Blood-orange Sorbet
Chocolate Sorbet
Redcurrant Sherbet
Peach, Apple & Strawberry Lollies

# Chocolate Ice Cream

**Serves 4**
**Preparation time 20 minutes,**
  **plus cooling and freezing**
**Cooking time 10 minutes**

300 ml (½ pint) double cream
2 tablespoons milk
50 g (2 oz) icing sugar, sifted
½ teaspoon vanilla extract
125 g (4 oz) good-quality
  plain dark chocolate,
  broken into pieces
2 tablespoons single cream
1 quantity easy peasy
  chocolate sauce (see
  page 186) (optional)

Put the double cream and milk in a bowl and whisk until just stiff. Stir in the icing sugar and vanilla extract. Pour the mixture into a shallow freezer container and freeze for 30 minutes or until the ice cream begins to set around the edges.

Melt the chocolate (see page 8), together with the single cream, over a pan of gently simmering water. Stir until smooth, then set aside to cool.

Remove the ice cream from the freezer and spoon into a bowl. Add the melted chocolate and quickly stir it through the ice cream with a fork. Return the ice cream to the freezer container, cover and freeze until set. Transfer the ice cream to the refrigerator 30 minutes before serving, to soften slightly.

Serve scoops of the ice cream with warm chocolate sauce (if using).

# Old-fashioned Vanilla Ice Cream

**Serves 6**
**Preparation time 10 minutes,**
**plus cooling and freezing**
**Cooking time 25 minutes**

300 ml (½ pint) single cream
1 vanilla pod
4 egg yolks
50 g (2 oz) caster sugar
300 ml (½ pint) double or
  whipping cream

Put the single cream and vanilla pod in a heavy-based saucepan, set over a low heat and bring to just below boiling. Remove from the heat and leave to infuse.

Place the egg yolks and sugar into a heatproof bowl and set over a pan of gently simmering water. Stir with a wooden spoon until thick and creamy, then gradually stir in the scalded single cream, removing the vanilla pod. Continue stirring for 15 minutes until the custard coats the spoon. Remove the bowl from the heat, cover with a circle of greaseproof paper to stop a skin from forming and leave to cool.

Pour the vanilla mixture into a freezer container, cover and transfer to the freezer for about 45 minutes or until slushy. Whip the cream until it just holds its shape. Remove the vanilla mixture from the freezer, beat thoroughly, then fold in the cream. Return the mixture to the container, cover and freeze for a further 45 minutes, then beat again until smooth. Freeze the ice cream for 1–2 hours.

Transfer the ice cream to the refrigerator for about 30 minutes to soften slightly before serving.

# Brown Bread Ice Cream

Serves 6–8
**Preparation time 20 minutes,**
**plus cooling and freezing**
**Cooking time 5 minutes**

75 g (3 oz) wholemeal
    breadcrumbs
50 g (2 oz) demerara sugar
50 g (2 oz) hazelnuts, skinned
    and ground
3 egg whites
125 g (4 oz) caster sugar
450 ml (¾ pint) double cream,
    lightly whipped
18 hazelnuts, to decorate

Combine the breadcrumbs, demerara sugar and ground hazelnuts on a heatproof plate. Place under a preheated hot grill until golden brown, stirring occasionally. Leave to cool.

Whisk the egg whites until stiff, then gradually whisk in the caster sugar. Fold two-thirds of the cream and the breadcrumb mixture into the egg white mixture. Turn into a 1.2 litre (2 pint) freezer-proof mould. Cover and freeze until solid.

Turn out onto a plate 30 minutes before serving. Decorate around the base with the remaining cream and the hazelnuts. Leave in the refrigerator to soften until required.

# Cherry Almond Ice Cream

**Serves 6**
**Preparation time 20 minutes,**
**plus cooling and freezing**
**Cooking time 20 minutes**

150 ml (¼ pint) milk
50 g (2 oz) ground almonds
1 egg
1 egg yolk
75 g (3 oz) caster sugar
2–3 drops almond extract
500 g (1 lb) red cherries,
    pitted, or cherry compôte
25 g (1 oz) slivered almonds
150 ml (¼ pint) double cream

Pour the milk into a small saucepan and stir in the ground almonds. Bring to the boil, then set aside.

Put the egg and the yolk into a heatproof bowl with the sugar and beat until pale and thick. Pour on the milk and almond mixture. Place the bowl over a pan of gently simmering water and stir until thick. Stir in the almond extract and leave to cool.

Purée the cherries in a food processor or blender (or use cherry compôte), then stir into the custard.

Toss the slivered almonds in a heavy pan over a low heat to toast them. Leave to cool.

Whip the cream until it forms soft peaks. Fold the whipped cream into the cherry mixture.

Transfer the mixture to a freezer container, cover and freeze until firm, beating twice at hourly intervals. Stir the slivered almonds into the mixture at the last beating. Serve the ice cream in individual glasses.

# Neapolitan Whirl Ice Cream

**Serves 8**
**Preparation time 20 minutes,**
  **plus cooling and freezing**
**Cooking time 5 minutes**

225 g (7½ oz) raspberries
175 g (6 oz) caster sugar
150 ml (¼ pint) water
200 g (7 oz) plain dark
  chocolate
600 ml (1 pint) double cream

Press the raspberries through a sieve to make a purée. Heat the sugar and measurement water in a pan until the sugar dissolves. Bring to the boil and boil for 2 minutes until syrupy. Leave to cool.

Melt the chocolate with 150 ml (¼ pint) of the cream in a bowl over a pan of simmering water (see page 8). Stir until smooth, then allow to cool slightly. Whip the remaining cream with the cooled syrup until the mixture is softly peaking.

Spoon half the cream and syrup mixture into a separate bowl and fold in the raspberry purée. Half-fold the chocolate mixture into the remaining cream and syrup mixture until marbled.

Put alternate spoonfuls of the raspberry and chocolate mixtures in a freezer container. Using a large metal spoon, fold the mixtures together 2 or 3 times until slightly mingled. Freeze overnight until firm.

Transfer the ice cream to the refrigerator about 30 minutes before serving.

# Rum & Raisin Ice Cream

**Serves 8**
**Preparation time 20 minutes,**
**plus cooling and freezing**
**Cooking time 15 minutes**

75 g (3 oz) seedless raisins
4 tablespoons dark rum
3 egg yolks
125 g (4 oz) soft brown sugar
300 ml (½ pint) single cream
300 ml (½ pint) double cream,
   lightly whipped

Place the rum and raisins in a small bowl and leave to soak.

Place the egg yolks and sugar in a heatproof bowl and whisk, using an electric beater, until thick and mousse-like. Put the single cream in a heavy-based saucepan, set over a low heat and bring to just below boiling. Stir into the egg mixture.

Set the bowl of egg mixture over a pan of gently simmering water. Stir with a wooden spoon until thick and creamy and the custard coats the spoon. Remove the bowl from the heat and strain the custard into a clean bowl. Cover with a circle of greaseproof paper to stop a skin from forming and leave to cool.

Fold the whipped double cream into the cooled custard. Turn the mixture into a freezer container, cover and freeze for 2–3 hours or until there is 2.5 cm (1 inch) of solid ice cream around the edges. Transfer to a bowl and mix well until smooth, then stir in the rum and raisins. Return to the freezer container, replace in the freezer and refreeze until firm.

Before serving, transfer the ice cream to the refrigerator for about 30 minutes to soften slightly.

# Lavender Honey Ice Cream

**Serves 4**
**Preparation time 20 minutes,
  plus chilling and freezing**
**Cooking time 15 minutes**

6 tablespoons lavender honey
  (or mild flower honey plus
  flowers from 8 lavender
  sprigs)
4 egg yolks
1 tablespoon cornflour
1 tablespoon caster sugar
300 ml (½ pint) milk
300 ml (½ pint) whipping
  cream

Put the honey, egg yolks, cornflour and sugar into a bowl and whisk lightly to combine. Bring the milk to the boil in a heavy-based saucepan. Pour the milk over the egg yolk mixture, whisking well to combine. Return the mixture to the saucepan and cook very gently, stirring constantly, until the custard has thickened enough to coat the back of the spoon thinly. Transfer to a bowl and cover with a circle of greaseproof paper to stop a skin from forming. Leave to cool, then chill in the refrigerator until very cold.

Lightly whip the cream and gently fold it into the custard (with the lavender flowers if using mild flower honey). Turn the mixture into a freezer container, cover and freeze until it has frozen around the edges. Transfer to a bowl and whisk lightly. Return to the freezer container, replace in the freezer and refreeze until the mixture is once again frozen around the edges. Repeat the whisking and freezing once or twice more.

Transfer the ice cream to the refrigerator for about 30 minutes to soften slightly before serving.

# Fresh Fruit Lollies

**Serves 8**
**Preparation time 20 minutes,**
**  plus freezing**
**Cooking time 15 minutes**

300 g (10 oz) fresh raspberries
25 g (1 oz) caster sugar
150 ml (¼ pint) water, plus
4 tablespoons
400 g (13 oz) can peaches in
  natural juice

Place the raspberries and sugar in a small pan with
4 tablespoons of the measurement water and bring to
the boil, stirring well until the sugar dissolves. Add the
remaining measurement water.

Put the raspberry liquid through a sieve, pressing down
well with a metal spoon to make as much of the pulp go
through as possible, only discarding the seeds.

Pour the mixture into 8 lolly moulds, filling just the base of
each. (Try using 8 rinsed yogurt pots placed in a roasting
tin. Cover with foil and push lolly sticks through the foil
into the centre of each pot. The foil will help secure the
stick in the centre.) Freeze for 1–2 hours until firm.

Meanwhile, put the peaches and juice into a food processor
and whiz until smooth. Once the raspberry base is firm,
pour the peach liquid over the top of the raspberry mixture
and freeze for a further 1–2 hours or overnight until firm.

# Strawberry Ice Cream

**Serves 6**
**Preparation time 15 minutes,**
**plus freezing**

500 g (1 lb) strawberries,
  hulled
4 tablespoons fresh orange
  juice
175 g (6 oz) caster sugar
450 ml (¾ pint) whipping
  cream

Finely mash the strawberries and mix with the orange juice to form a smooth purée. Stir in the sugar.

Whip the cream until it forms soft peaks and fold into the purée. Pour the mixture into a 1 kg (2 lb) loaf tin. Freeze for 1½ hours or until partly frozen.

Turn the mixture into a bowl, break it up with a fork and then whisk until smooth. Return the mixture to the loaf tin and freeze for 5 hours until it is completely frozen.

Transfer the ice cream to the refrigerator for about 30 minutes to soften slightly before serving.

# Summer Berry Sorbet

**Serves 2**
**Preparation time 5 minutes,
  plus freezing**

250 g (8 oz) frozen mixed
   summer berries
75 ml (3 fl oz) spiced berry
   cordial
2 tablespoons kirsch
1 tablespoon lime juice

Put a shallow plastic container in the freezer to chill.
Process the frozen berries, cordial, kirsch and lime juice
in a food processor or blender to a smooth purée. Be
careful not to over-process, as this will soften the mixture
too much.

Spoon into the chilled container and freeze for at least
25 minutes. Spoon into serving bowls and serve.

# Lemon Sorbet

Serves 4
Preparation time 15 minutes,
  plus plus cooling and
  freezing

125 g (4 oz) caster sugar
5 tablespoons boiling water
500 ml (17 fl oz) freshly
  squeezed lemon juice
  (about 10 lemons)
lemon rind curls, to decorate

Put the sugar in a heatproof jug. Pour over the measurement water and stir until the sugar has started to dissolve. Pour in the lemon juice and stir well until all the sugar has dissolved.

Pour the mixture into a shallow freezerproof container and cover with clingfilm.

Place in the freezer and freeze for 45 minutes. Remove from the freezer and beat with a whisk to break up the ice crystals. Return to the freezer and repeat once or twice more at 45-minute intervals, until almost completely frozen. Process the sorbet in a food processor or blender until smooth. Freeze until solid.

Transfer to the refrigerator 10 minutes before serving to soften slightly. Serve in individual bowls or glasses, decorated with lemon rind curls and accompanied by shortbread biscuits. The sorbet is best eaten on the day it is made.

# Blood-orange Sorbet

Serves 4–6
**Preparation time** 25 minutes, plus chilling and freezing
**Cooking time** 20 minutes

250 g (8 oz) caster sugar
250 ml (8 fl oz) water
pared rind of 2 blood oranges
300 ml (½ pint) blood orange juice
chilled Campari, to serve (optional)
orange rind, to decorate

Heat the sugar over a low heat in a small saucepan with the measurement water, stirring occasionally until completely dissolved. Add the orange rind and increase the heat. Without stirring, boil the syrup for about 12 minutes and then set aside to cool completely.

When it is cold, strain the sugar syrup over the orange juice and stir together.

Pour the chilled orange syrup into a shallow metal container and put it in the freezer for 2 hours. Remove and whisk with a hand-held electric whisk or balloon whisk, breaking up all the ice crystals. Return it to the freezer and repeat this process every hour or so until frozen.

Serve scoops of sorbet with a splash of chilled Campari, if liked, and decorate with thin strips of orange rind.

# Chocolate Sorbet

**Serves 6**
**Preparation time 5 minutes,**
**plus cooling and freezing**
**Cooking time 15 minutes**

200 g (7 oz) dark muscovado
  sugar
50 g (2 oz) cocoa powder
1 teaspoon instant espresso
  coffee powder
1 cinnamon stick
600 ml (1 pint) water
12 chocolate coffee
  matchsticks
2 tablespoons chocolate
  liqueur, to serve

Mix the sugar, cocoa powder, coffee and cinnamon stick in a large pan with the measurement water. Slowly bring to the boil, stirring until the sugar has dissolved, boil for 5 minutes, then take off the heat. Leave to cool. Remove the cinnamon stick.

Pour the cooled liquid into a freezer-proof container, seal and freeze for 2–4 hours until firm. Whiz in a food processor until smooth, then pour into a 1 kg (2 lb) loaf tin and freeze for 2 hours or until frozen solid.

Turn out on to a serving plate and arrange the coffee matchsticks over the top to decorate. Cut into slices to serve and drizzle 1 teaspoon chocolate liqueur around each portion.

# Redcurrant Sherbet

**Serves 4**
**Preparation time 20 minutes,**
  **plus freezing**

500 g (1 lb) redcurrants
125 g (4 oz) icing sugar, sifted
juice of 1 orange
1 egg white

Place the redcurrants, icing sugar and orange juice in a liquidizer or food processor and blend to a purée. Sieve to remove the pips.

Turn the mixture into a freezer container, cover and freeze for 2–3 hours or slushy. Turn the mixture into a bowl, break it up with a fork and then whisk until smooth.

Whisk the egg white until stiff, then whisk into the half-frozen purée. Return the mixture to the freezer container, replace in the freezer and freeze until firm.

Transfer the ice cream to the refrigerator for about 15 minutes to soften slightly before serving.

# Peach, Apple & Strawberry Lollies

**Makes 4**
**Preparation time 7–8**
 **minutes, plus freezing**

2 peaches, peeled, stoned
 and cut into chunks
300 ml (½ pint) water
1 red apple, peeled
125 g (4 oz) strawberries,
 hulled

Place the peaches in a blender and whiz until smooth. Add one-third of the measurement water and divide evenly between 4 lolly moulds. Freeze until just set.

Chop the apples into even-sized chunks and juice them. Add one-third of the water and pour on top of the frozen peach mixture, then freeze until just set.

Hull the strawberries and juice them. Add the remainder of the water and pour on top of the frozen apple mixture, then freeze until set.

# Family Favourites

Quick Lemon Meringue Pie
Chocolate Bread & Butter Pudding
Strawberry, Pear & Apple Crumble
Brown Betty
Pancake Stack with Maple Syrup
Berry Eton Mess
Banoffi Pie
Toffee Peaches
Spiced Bananas
Sticky Toffee Puddings
Topsy-turvy Banana Ginger Pudding
Apple & Sultana Pots
Chocolate, Pear & Orange Pudding
Raspberry Ripple Meringues

# Quick Lemon Meringue Pie

Serves 6
Preparation time 15 minutes
Cooking time 15–20 minutes

20 cm (8 inch) shop-bought
    sweet pastry case
400 g (13 oz) can condensed
    milk
2 eggs yolks
grated rind and juice of
    2 lemons

**Meringue**
4 egg whites
200 g (7 oz) caster sugar

Place the pastry case on a baking sheet. Place the condensed milk, egg yolks and lemon rind and juice in a large bowl and beat together. Pour into the pastry case to 1 cm (½ inch) below the top.

Whisk the egg whites in a clean large bowl with a hand-held electric whisk until they form soft peaks, then gradually whisk in the sugar until the mixture is thick and glossy (see page 9).

Pile the meringue on top of the lemon mixture and place in a preheated oven, 190°C (375°F), Gas Mark 5, for 15–20 minutes until golden and crisp.

# Chocolate Bread & Butter Pudding

Serves 4
Preparation time 10 minutes
Cooking time 20 minutes

25 g (1 oz) unsalted butter,
  softened
100 g (3½ oz) milk chocolate,
  broken into small pieces
12 slices of fruit loaf
500 g (1 lb) pot fresh custard
100 ml (3½ fl oz) milk
25 g (1 oz) sultanas
2 tablespoons demerara
  sugar

Grease a 1 litre (1¾ pint) ovenproof dish.

Melt the chocolate in a heatproof bowl set over a saucepan of gently simmering water (see page 8). Meanwhile, butter each slice of bread, then cut in half diagonally, forming triangles.

Place the custard in a jug and stir in the melted chocolate. Make up the custard to 600 g (1 lb 3½ oz) with the milk.

Arrange a layer of bread in the bottom of the prepared dish. Sprinkle with the sultanas, then place the remaining bread on top. Pour over the chocolate custard and leave to stand for 5 minutes.

Sprinkle with the sugar and place in a preheated oven, 180°C (350°F), Gas Mark 4, for 20 minutes or until bubbling.

# Strawberry, Pear & Apple Crumble

Serves 8
Preparation time 30 minutes
Cooking time 45–50 minutes

500 g (1 lb) eating apples,
   peeled, cored and roughly
   chopped
250 g (8 oz) pears, peeled,
   cored and roughly chopped
finely grated rind and juice of
   1 orange
4 tablespoons clear honey
½ teaspoon ground ginger
175 g (6 oz) strawberries,
   hulled and quartered

**Crumble**
50 g (2 oz) plain flour
3 tablespoons cold-milled
   flaxseed (ground linseed)
50 g (2 oz) butter, cubed
50 g (2 oz) porridge oats
50 g (2 oz) mixed seeds (such
   as pumpkin, sunflower,
   sesame and hemp)
75 g (3 oz) demerara sugar

Place the apples and pears in a medium, heavy-based saucepan with the orange rind and juice, honey and ginger. Bring to a gentle simmer, stirring occasionally, then cover and simmer for 10 minutes until soft and slightly pulpy. Add the strawberries and cook for a further 2–3 minutes until soft, yet still retaining their shape. Remove the pan from the heat and transfer the mixture to an ovenproof gratin dish. Set aside while making the crumble.

Put the flour in a bowl and stir in the flaxseed. Add the butter and rub into the mixture until it resembles chunky breadcrumbs. Add the oats and again rub the fat into the mixture using your fingertips to distribute well. Stir in the seeds and sugar then sprinkle over the fruit.

Bake in a preheated oven, 200°C (400°F), Gas Mark 6, for 30–35 minutes until the topping is golden. Serve the crumble warm.

# Brown Betty

**Serves 6**
**Preparation time 20 minutes**
**Cooking time 40 minutes**

10 slices white bread, crusts
   removed
75 g (3 oz) unsalted butter,
   softened
1 kg (2 lb) cooking apples,
   peeled, cored and sliced
75 g (3 oz) soft brown sugar

Spread the bread thickly with the butter and cut each slice into 4 squares. Butter a 1.5 litre (2½ pint) ovenproof dish generously and line with some of the bread, butter-side down.

Cover with half the apples, sprinkle with sugar and arrange another layer of bread over the top. Cover with remaining apples, sprinkle with sugar and top with the remaining bread, butter-side up and slightly overlapping. Sprinkle with the remaining sugar.

Cover with foil and bake in a preheated oven, 180˚C (350˚F), Gas Mark 4, for 35 minutes. Remove the foil and bake for a further 5 minutes until crisp and golden. Serve hot with custard or cream.

# Pancake Stack with Maple Syrup

Serves 4
Preparation time 10 minutes
Cooking time 6 minutes

1 egg
100 g (3½ oz) plain flour
125 ml (4 fl oz) milk
2½ tablespoons vegetable oil
1 tablespoon caster sugar
maple syrup, to drizzle

Put the egg, flour, milk, oil and sugar in a food processor or blender and whiz until smooth and creamy.

Heat a large frying pan over a medium heat and put in 4 half-ladlefuls of the batter to make 4 pancakes. After about 1 minute the tops of the pancakes will start to set and air bubbles will rise to the top and burst. Use a spatula to turn the pancakes over and cook on the other side for 1 minute. Repeat twice more until you have used all the batter and made 12 small pancakes in all.

Bring the pancakes to the table as a stack, drizzled with maple syrup, and serve 3 pancakes to each person, with scoops of ice cream.

# Berry Eton Mess

**Serves 6**
**Preparation time 10 minutes,**
  **plus cooling**
**Cooking time 1 hour**

3 egg whites
250 g (8 oz) caster sugar
1 teaspoon white wine
  vinegar
300 ml (½ pint) double cream
200 g (7 oz) raspberries,
  plus extra, left whole, to
  decorate
200 g (7 oz) strawberries,
  hulled and quartered,
  plus extra, left whole and
  unhulled, to decorate
2 tablespoons icing sugar
2 tablespoons cream liqueur

Line 2 large baking sheets with nonstick baking paper.

Whisk the egg whites in a large clean bowl until they form stiff peaks. Add the sugar a spoonful at a time and continue to whisk until thick and glossy (see page 9). Fold in the vinegar with a large metal spoon.

Spoon or pipe 12 meringues on to the prepared baking sheets. Place in a preheated oven, 150°C (300°F), Gas Mark 2, for 1 hour, then switch off the oven and leave the meringues to cool completely. When cool, roughly crush the meringues.

Whip the cream in a large bowl until it forms soft peaks. Roughly crush together the raspberries and strawberries and stir into the cream. Fold in the crushed meringues, icing sugar and cream liqueur. Spoon into 6 tall glasses, decorate with extra whole berries, and serve immediately.

# Banoffi Pie

Serves 6
Preparation time 15 minutes,
    plus chilling
Cooking time 10 minutes

250 g (8 oz) digestive biscuits
250 g (8 oz) butter
125 g (4 oz) light muscovado
    sugar
400 g (13 oz) can condensed
    milk
2 bananas
1 tablespoon lemon juice
250 ml (8 fl oz) whipping
    cream
25 g (1 oz) chocolate curls
    (see page 8)

Crush the digestive biscuits in a clean plastic bag with a rolling pin or wine bottle or process in a food processor to make fine crumbs.

Melt 125 g (4 oz) of the butter in a saucepan and stir in the crumbs. Press the biscuit mix evenly over the base and sides of a deep 20 cm (8 inch) round springform tin or similar. Put in the refrigerator for 1 hour.

Make the filling. Put the remaining butter and sugar in a saucepan over a low heat. Once the butter has melted, stir in the condensed milk and bring slowly to the boil. Turn down the heat and simmer for 5 minutes, stirring all the time, until the mixture turns a caramel colour. Pour on to the biscuit base and chill in the refrigerator for about 1 hour, until the mixture has set.

Slice the bananas and toss in the lemon juice. Keep a quarter of the bananas for the top and spread the rest over the filling.

Whip the cream until it forms soft peaks and spoon it over the top. Decorate with the rest of the banana slices and sprinkle with the chocolate shavings.

# Toffee Peaches

Serves 4
Preparation time 10 minutes
Cooking time 15 minutes

4 peaches, halved and stoned
50 g (2 oz) ground almonds

**Sauce**
125 (4 oz) soft light brown
    sugar
5 tablespoons maple syrup
25 g (1 oz) butter
150 ml (¼ pint) single cream

Cut 4 x 20 cm (8 inch) square pieces of foil and place 2 peach halves in each. Sprinkle over the ground almonds. Scrunch up the foil to form 4 parcels and place under a preheated medium grill or 5–8 minutes, turning once or twice during cooking until the peaches are soft.

Meanwhile, make the sauce. Place the sugar, maple syrup and butter in a nonstick saucepan over a moderately low heat until the sugar dissolves. Stir continuously until the sauce boils and thickens, which should take about 3 minutes. Add the cream and return to the boil, then immediately remove from the heat.

Drizzle the sauce over the peaches, and serve.

# Spiced Bananas

Serves 8
Preparation time 10 minutes
Cooking time 10 minutes

8 bananas, peeled
2 tablespoons lemon juice
8 tablespoons light
  muscavado sugar
50 g (2 oz) butter, softened
1 teaspoon cinnamon

**Rum mascarpone cream**
250 g (8 oz) mascarpone
  cheese
2 tablespoons rum
1–2 tablespoons granulated
  sugar

Put each banana on a double piece of foil. Drizzle over the lemon juice and sprinkle 1 tablespoon of the brown sugar on each banana.

Beat together the butter and cinnamon in a bowl until creamy, then spoon over the bananas. Wrap each banana tightly in the foil and cook over a barbecue or under a preheated medium grill for 10 minutes.

Meanwhile, make the rum mascarpone cream. Mix together the mascarpone, rum and sugar in a bowl.

Unwrap the bananas and slice thickly. Serve immediately with the rum mascarpone cream.

# Sticky Toffee Puddings

**Serves 4**
**Preparation time 10 minutes**
**Cooking time 25–30 minutes**

2 tablespoons golden syrup
2 tablespoons black treacle
150 g (5 oz) butter, softened
2 tablespoons double cream
125 g (4 oz) caster sugar
2 eggs, beaten
100 g (3½ oz) self-raising flour
50 g (2 oz) walnuts, lightly
   toasted and ground

Lightly oil 4 x 200 ml (7 fl oz) ramekins. In a small saucepan, heat together the golden syrup, treacle and 50 g (2 oz) of the butter until melted. Divide half the mixture between the prepared ramekins, stir double cream into the remainder and set aside.

Put the remaining butter and sugar in a food processor and process briefly. Add the eggs and flour and process again for 30 seconds. Stir in the walnuts.

Spoon the sponge mixture into the ramekins to cover the syrup mixture.

Stand the ramekins in a shallow roasting tin and bake in a preheated oven, 180°C (350°F), Gas Mark 4, for 25–30 minutes until risen and golden.

Remove the ramekins from the oven and leave to stand for 5 minutes. Meanwhile, heat the remaining treacle mixture. Unmould the puddings and pour over the treacle. Serve with custard or cream.

# Topsy-turvy Banana Ginger Pudding

Serves 6
Preparation time 25 minutes
Cooking time 30 minutes

4 tablespoons golden syrup,
  plus extra to serve
4 tablespoons light
  muscovado sugar
3 large bananas, halved
  lengthways
juice of 1 lemon

**Ginger pudding**
100 g (3½ oz) unsalted butter
100 g (3½ oz) light
  muscovado sugar
75 g (3 oz) golden syrup, plus
  extra for drizzling
2 eggs
4 tablespoons milk
175 g (6 oz) wholemeal plain
  flour
1 teaspoon bicarbonate of
  soda
2 teaspoons ground ginger

Grease a roasting tin with a base measurement of
23 x 18 cm (9 x 7 inches), and line the base with nonstick
baking paper. Spoon the syrup and sugar into the base.
Toss the bananas in the lemon juice, then arrange cut side
downwards in the tin.

Heat the butter, sugar and syrup for the ginger pudding
gently in a medium saucepan, stirring until melted. Take
the pan off the heat.

Beat the eggs and milk in a jug, then mix the flour,
bicarbonate of soda and ginger in a bowl. Gradually stir the
milk mixture into the pan of melted butter, then stir in the
flour mix and beat until smooth.

Pour the mixture over the bananas, then bake in a
preheated oven, 180°C (350°F), Gas Mark 4, for
30 minutes until well risen and the centre springs back
when pressed.

Leave to cool for 5 minutes, then loosen the edge and
invert the tin on to a large plate with a rim. Remove the
tin and lining paper, then cut the pudding into portions.
Serve drizzled with a little extra syrup and custard or cream.

# Apple & Sultana Pots

Serves 4
Preparation time 15 minutes
Cooking time 15–20 minutes

2 lapsang souchong tea bags
100 ml (3½ fl oz) boiling water
1 tablespoon clear honey
3 tablespoons sultanas
3 dessert or cooking apples,
  peeled, cored and diced
½ teaspoon mixed spice
25 g (1 oz) dark brown sugar
25 g (1 oz) unsalted butter
150 g (5 oz) double cream,
  whipped to soft peaks
caster sugar, to sprinkle

Make a strong infusion of tea using the teabags in the measurement boiling water. Stir in the honey and sultanas and set aside to infuse.

Put the apples in a saucepan with the mixed spice, brown sugar and butter. Remove the teabags from the infusion and pour the liquid over the apples.

Cover and cook over a medium-low heat, stirring frequently, for 15–20 minutes until the apples start to collapse. Crush to a chunky purée.

Stir the double cream into the apple purée until well combine, then spoon the mixture into 4 individual ovenproof dishes.

Sprinkle the surface generously with caster sugar, then place the dishes under a hot grill until the sugar begins to caramelize. Serve warm or cold with ginger snaps.

# Chocolate, Pear & Orange Pudding

**Serves 8**
**Preparation time 25 minutes**
**Cooking time 30–35 minutes**

175 g (6 oz) butter, at room
   temperature
175 g (6 oz) caster sugar
3 eggs, beaten
125 g (4 oz) self-raising flour
75 g (3 oz) self-raising
   wholemeal flour
25 g (1 oz) cocoa
grated rind and 2
   tablespoons juice from
   1 orange
4 small conference pears,
   peeled, halved and cored

**To finish**
sifted icing sugar, for dusting
a little grated chocolate
a little grated orange rind

Beat the butter and sugar together in a mixing bowl until light and fluffy. Gradually mix in alternate spoonfuls of beaten egg and flour until all has been added and the mixture is smooth. Stir in the cocoa, orange rind and juice then spoon the mixture into an 18 x 28 cm (7 x 11 inch) roasting tin lined with nonstick baking paper, and spread the surface level.

Cut each pear half into long thin slices and fan out slightly but keep together in their original shape. Carefully lift on to the top of the pudding and arrange in 2 rows of 4.

Bake in a preheated oven, 180°C (350°F), Gas Mark 4, for 30–35 minutes until well risen and the pudding springs back when gently pressed with a fingertip.

Lift out of the tin using the lining paper, cut into 8 pieces and peel off the paper. Dust with sifted icing sugar and sprinkle with a little extra grated chocolate and orange rind. Serve warm with ice cream or custard.

# Raspberry Ripple Meringues

❦❦❦

**Makes about 12**
**Preparation time 15 minutes**
**Cooking time 1¼ hours**

40 g (1½ oz) fresh raspberries,
   plus extra to serve
2 tablespoons raspberry jam
4 egg whites
200 g (7 oz) caster sugar

Put the raspberries in a bowl and mash with a fork until broken up and turning juicy. Add the jam and mash together to make a purée. Tip into a sieve resting over a small bowl and press the purée with the back of a spoon to extract as much juice as possible.

Whisk the egg whites in a large clean bowl with a hand-held electric whisk until peaking. Whisk in a tablespoonful of the sugar and continue to whisk for about 15 seconds. Gradually add the remaining sugar, a spoonful at a time, until thick and glossy (see page 9).

Drizzle over the raspberry purée and lightly stir in using a spatula or large metal spoon, scooping up the meringue from the base of the bowl so that the mixture is streaked with the purée. Take care not to over-mix.

Drop large spoonfuls of the mixture, each about the size of a small orange, on to a large baking sheet lined with baking parchment, then swirl with the back of a teaspoon. Bake in a preheated oven, 120°C (250°F), Gas Mark ½, for about 1¼ hours or until the meringues are crisp and come away easily from the paper. Leave to cool on the paper. Serve with extra raspberries and cream.

# A Slice of Pie

Peach Melba Pie
Apricot Tartlets
Pear & Almond Tart
Plum & Marzipan Slice
French Apple Flans
Tiny Treacle Tarts
Deep Dish Citrus Apple Pies
Sweet Cherry Pies
Autumn Fruit Pies
Blackcurrant Flan
Caramel, Pear & Marzipan Tart
Prune & Custard Tart
Summer Berry Tarts

# Peach Melba Pie

**Serves 6**
**Preparation time 40 minutes,**
   **plus cooling**
**Cooking time 30–35 minutes**

1 quantity sweet shortcrust
   pastry (see page 7)
75 g (3 oz) caster sugar, plus
   extra for sprinkling
1 teaspoon cornflour
grated rind of 1 lemon
750 g (1½ lb) peaches, halved,
   stoned, sliced
150 g (5 oz) raspberries
milk, to glaze

Reserve one-third of the pastry for the lattice. Roll out the remainder on a lightly floured surface until large enough to line the base and sides of a buttered metal pie dish, 20 cm (8 inches) in diameter and 5 cm (2 inches) deep. Lift the pastry over a rolling pin, drape into the dish, then press over the base and sides (see page 6).

Mix the sugar, cornflour and lemon rind together, then add the fruits and toss together gently. Pile into the pie dish. Trim off the excess pastry, add to the reserved portion, then roll out. Cut into 1.5 cm (¾ inch) wide strips long enough to go over the top of the pie.

Brush the top edge of the pie with milk and arrange the pastry strips over the top as a lattice. Trim off the excess. Brush with milk, then sprinkle with a little sugar.

Bake in a preheated oven, 190°C (375°F), Gas Mark 5, for 30–35 minutes until golden. Leave to cool for 15 minutes, then serve cut into wedges.

# Apricot Tartlets

Serves 4
**Preparation time** 15 minutes
**Cooking time** 20–25 minutes

375 g (12 oz) ready-rolled puff
    pastry, defrosted if frozen
100 g (3½ oz) marzipan
12 canned apricot halves,
    drained
light muscovado sugar, for
    sprinkling
apricot jam, for glazing

Using a saucer as a template, cut 4 rounds from the pastry, each approximately 8 cm (3½ inches) in diameter. Score a line about 1 cm (½ inch) from the edge of each round with a sharp knife.

Roll out the marzipan to 2.5 mm (⅛ inch) thick and cut out 4 rounds to fit inside the scored circles. Lay the pastry rounds on a baking sheet, place a circle of marzipan in the centre of each and arrange 3 apricot halves, cut-side up, on top. Sprinkle a little sugar into each apricot.

Put the baking sheet on top of a second preheated baking sheet (this helps to crisp the pastry bases) and bake in a preheated oven, 200°C (400°F), Gas Mark 6, for 20–25 minutes until the pastry is puffed and browned and the apricots are slightly caramelized around the edges. While still hot, brush the tops with apricot jam to glaze. Serve immediately.

# Pear & Almond Tart

**Serves 8**
**Preparation time 20 minutes,**
  **plus chilling**
**Cooking time 50–55 minutes**

450 g (14½ oz) chilled
  ready-made or homemade
  sweet shortcrust pastry (see
  page 7)
125 g (4 oz) unsalted butter,
  softened
125 g (4 oz) caster sugar
125 g (4 oz) ground almonds
2 eggs, lightly beaten
1 tablespoon lemon juice
3 ripe pears, peeled, cored
  and thickly sliced
25 g (1 oz) flaked almonds
icing sugar, for dusting

Roll out the pastry on a lightly floured surface and use it to line a 25 cm (10 inch) flan tin (see page 6). Prick the base with a fork and chill for 30 minutes. Line with nonstick baking paper, add macaroni or beans and bake blind (see page 7) in a preheated oven, 190°C (375°F), Gas Mark 5, for 15 minutes. Remove the baking paper and macaroni or beans and bake for a further 5–10 minutes until the pastry is crisp and golden. Leave to cool completely. Reduce the temperature to 190°C (375°F), Gas Mark 5.

Beat the butter, sugar and ground almonds together until smooth, then beat in the eggs and lemon juice.

Arrange the pear slices over the pastry case and carefully spread over the almond mixture. Sprinkle with the flaked almonds and bake for 30 minutes until the topping is golden and firm to the touch. Remove from the oven and leave to cool.

Dust the tart with sifted icing sugar and serve in wedges with easy peasy chocolate sauce (see page 186) and a scoop of vanilla ice cream.

# Plum & Marzipan Slice

**Serves 8**
**Preparation time 15 minutes**
**Cooking time 25 minutes**

500 g (1 lb) ready-made puff
    pastry
250 g (8 oz) marzipan
800 g (1 lb 10 oz) plums,
    halved and stoned
beaten egg, to glaze

**Glaze**
3 tablespoons smooth
    apricot jam
1 teaspoon rosewater
2 teaspoons water

Roll out the pastry on a lightly floured surface to a 35 x 20 cm (14 x 8 inch) rectangle. Place on a greased baking sheet. Using a sharp knife, score a 1.5 cm (¾ inch) border around the pastry edge. Roll out the marzipan on a surface lightly dusted with icing sugar to a 30 x 15 cm (12 x 6 inch) rectangle, then place inside the border. Arrange the plums over the marzipan. Brush the pastry border with beaten egg.

Bake in a preheated oven, 200°C (400°F), Gas Mark 6, for about 25 minutes until the pastry is risen and golden and the plums are tender.

Meanwhile, heat the glaze ingredients in a small saucepan, then brush over the plums. Serve warm or cold.

# French Apple Flans

**Makes 4**
**Preparation time 20 minutes,**
  **plus chilling**
**Cooking time 25–30 minutes**

375 g (12 oz) ready-made puff
  pastry
2 crisp green dessert apples
  (such as Granny Smith),
  peeled, cored and sliced
1 tablespoon caster sugar
25 g (1 oz) unsalted butter,
  chilled

**Apricot glaze**
250 g (8 oz) apricot jam
2 teaspoons lemon juice
2 teaspoons water

Divide the pastry into quarters and roll each out on a
lightly floured surface until 2 mm (⅛ inch) thick. Using a
13 cm (5½ inch) plate as a guide, cut out 4 rounds – make
a number of short cuts around the plate rather than
drawing the knife around, which can stretch the pastry.
Place the rounds on a baking sheet.

Place a slightly smaller plate on each pastry round and
score around the edge to form a 1 cm (½ inch) border.
Prick the centres with a fork and chill for 30 minutes.

Arrange the apple slices in a circle over the pastry rounds
and sprinkle with the sugar. Grate the butter over the top
and bake in a preheated oven, 220°C (425°F), Gas Mark 7,
for 25–30 minutes until the pastry and apples are golden.

Meanwhile, make the apricot glaze. Put the jam in a small
saucepan with the lemon juice and water and heat gently
until the jam melts. Increase the heat and boil for 1 minute,
remove from the heat and press through a fine sieve. Keep
warm then brush over each apple tart while they are still
warm. Serve with ice cream.

# Tiny Treacle Tarts

**Makes 24**
**Preparation time 30 minutes,**
**plus chilling**
**Cooking time 25 minutes**

1 quantity pâte sucrée (see page 7)
50 g (2 oz) butter
75 g (3 oz) light muscovado sugar
300 g (10 oz) golden syrup
grated rind of 1 lemon
2 tablespoons lemon juice
1 egg, beaten
50 g (2 oz) fresh breadcrumbs

Roll the pastry out thinly on a lightly floured surface, then stamp out 24 × 6 cm (2½ inch) circles with a fluted biscuit cutter and press into the buttered sections of 2 × 12-section mini muffin tins. Reknead and reroll pastry trimmings as needed. Chill for 15 minutes.

Put the butter, sugar, syrup, lemon rind and juice in a small saucepan and cook over a low heat until the butter has just melted and the sugar dissolved. Take off the heat and leave to cool slightly.

Stir the beaten egg and breadcrumbs into the syrup mix and beat until smooth. Spoon into the pastry cases.

Bake in a preheated oven, 180°C (350°F), Gas Mark 4, for 15–20 minutes. Leave to cool for 15 minutes, then loosen the tarts with a knife and remove from the tins. Transfer to a wire rack and leave to cool slightly. Serve warm with spoonfuls of whipped cream sprinkled with ground cinnamon.

# Deep Dish Citrus Apple Pies

Makes 12
Preparation time 40 minutes
Cooking time 30 minutes

750 g (1½ lb) cooking apples,
    quartered, cored, peeled
    and sliced
grated rind and juice of
    1 lemon
50 g (2 oz) butter
100 g (3½ oz) caster sugar,
    plus extra for sprinkling
juice of ½ orange
1 tablespoon cornflour
50 g (2 oz) sultanas
1½ quantities sweet
    shortcrust pastry (see
    page 7)
beaten egg or milk, to glaze

Toss the apple slices in the lemon rind and juice. Heat the butter in a large frying pan, add the apples, sugar and orange rind and cook gently for 5 minutes until the apples are softened but still hold their shape.

Mix the cornflour with the orange juice, add to the pan with the sultanas and cook until the juices have thickened. Take off the heat and leave to cool.

Reserve one-third of the pastry, then roll out the remainder thinly on a lightly floured surface. Stamp out 12 × 10 cm (4 inch) circles with a plain biscuit cutter and press into a buttered 12-section muffin tin.

Spoon the apple filling into the pie cases, doming it up high in the centre. Roll out the reserved pastry and any pastry trimmings, then cut out 12 × 7 cm (3 inch) lids with a fluted biscuit cutter. Brush the pie edges with milk, then press the lids on the pies. Reroll the trimmings and cut small decorations. Brush the tops of the pies with milk, add the decorations and brush these with egg or milk, then sprinkle with a little caster sugar.

Bake in a preheated oven, 190°C (375°F), Gas Mark 5, for 25 minutes until the pastry is golden. Leave to stand in the tins for 20 minutes, then loosen the edges with a knife, lift out of the tins and serve warm with custard.

# Sweet Cherry Pies

Makes 4
Preparation time 30 minutes
Cooking time 20–25 minutes

125 g (4 oz) caster sugar, plus
    extra for sprinkling
1 tablespoon cornflour
½ teaspoon ground star anise
    or cinnamon
500 g (1 lb) frozen pitted
    black cherries, just
    defrosted, halved
1 quantity sweet shortcrust
    pastry (see page 7),
    flavoured with grated rind
    of ½ orange, chilled
milk or beaten egg, to glaze

Mix the sugar, cornflour and star anise or cinnamon together, then add the cherries and toss together.

Roll out two-thirds of the pastry thinly on a lightly floured surface. Use to line 4 fluted loose-bottomed 10 cm (4 inch) tart tins (see page 6), rerolling the pastry trimmings as needed. Spoon the cherry mixture into the pastry cases, and brush the top edges with milk or beaten egg. Roll out the reserved pastry with any trimmings and and cut 4 x 10 cm (4 inch) circles with a fluted biscuit cutter.

Add the pie lids and press the pastry edges together to seal. Slash the tops with a knife, then brush the tops with milk or beaten egg and sprinkle with a little extra sugar.

Bake in a preheated oven, 180°C (350°F), Gas Mark 4, for 20–25 minutes until the pastry is golden. Leave to stand for 15 minutes, then loosen the edges of the pies and take out of the tin. Serve warm or cold with custard.

# Autumn Fruit Pies

Makes 6
Preparation time 35 minutes,
  plus cooling
Cooking time 45–50 minutes

175 g (6 oz) blackcurrants
125 g (4 oz) caster sugar, plus
  extra for sprinkling
2 tablespoons water
1 tablespoon cornflour
1 teaspoon ground cinnamon,
  plus extra for sprinkling
grated rind of 1 orange
375 g (12 oz) ripe plums,
  stoned and diced
150 g (5 oz) blackberries
milk, to glaze

**Hot water crust pastry**
175 g (6 oz) lard
175 ml (6 fl oz) milk and water,
  mixed half and half
50 g (2 oz) caster sugar
375 g (12 oz) plain flour
¼ teaspoon salt

To make the pastry, place the lard and milk and water mix and sugar in a saucepan and heat gently until the lard has just melted. Bring just to the boil, then tip into a bowl containing the flour and salt and mix with a wooden spoon until it forms a smooth soft ball. Cover the top of the bowl with a clean cloth and leave to cool for 20 minutes.

Put the blackcurrants, sugar and water in a saucepan and heat for 5 minutes until soft. Mix the cornflour to a paste with a little extra water, add to the pan and cook, stirring until thickened. Take off the heat and stir in the cinnamon, orange rind, plums and blackberries. Set aside.

Reserve one-third of the pastry, then cut the remainder into 6 pieces. Press one piece over the base, up and slightly above the top of a 250 ml (8 fl oz) individual pudding mould. Repeat with 5 more moulds.

Spoon in the filling. Cut the reserved pastry into 6, then roll out each on a lightly floured surface to form lids. Cut small heart shapes in the centre of each lid. Place over the filling and press the edges together well. Trim off the excess pastry and flute the edges (see page 8). Brush with milk and sprinkle with extra sugar and cinnamon.

Put the moulds on a baking sheet, then bake in a preheated oven, 180°C (350°F), Gas Mark 4, for 40–45 minutes until golden. Cover with foil after 30 minutes. Leave to cool for 10 minutes, then serve in the moulds.

# Blackcurrant Flan

Serves 6
Preparation time 30 minutes,
  plus cooling and chilling
Cooking time 45–50 minutes

175 g (6 oz) plain flour
2 teaspoons ground
  cinnamon
124 g (4 oz) unsalted butter,
  diced
25 g (1 oz) caster sugar
1 egg yolk
2 teaspoons water
water and caster sugar, to
  glaze

**Filling**
500 g (1 lb) blackcurrants
125 g (4 oz) demerara sugar

Sift the flour and cinnamon together into a large bowl. Rub in the butter until the mixture resembles breadcrumbs. Stir in the caster sugar. Add the egg yolk and water and mix to a firm dough.

Knead lightly, then roll out thinly on a lightly floured surface and use to line an 18 cm (7 inch) flan tin (see page 6). Chill the flan and pastry trimmings for 15 minutes.

Put the blackcurrants and demerara sugar in a heavy-bottomed saucepan. Cover and cook gently for 10 minutes, then uncover, increase the heat and cook until thick and syrupy. Remove from the heat and turn onto a plate to cool.

Place the cooled fruit in the flan case. Roll out the pastry trimmings, cut into strips and make a lattice pattern over the fruit. Brush the pastry with water and sprinkle with caster sugar.

Bake in a preheated oven, 200°C (400°F), Gas Mark 6, for 25–30 minutes, until golden. Serve warm or cold, with whipped cream.

# Caramel, Pear & Marzipan Tart

Serves 8
Preparation time 10 minutes,
  plus cooling
Cooking time 45 minutes

50 g (2 oz) unsalted butter
50 g (2 oz) soft light brown
  sugar
6 ripe pears, peeled, halved
  and cored
25 g (1 oz) marzipan
25g (8 oz) ready-made
  shortcrust pastry or
  homemade sweet
  shortcrust pastry (see
  page 7)

Place the butter and sugar in a 22 cm (9 inch) fixed-bottomed cake tin. Place over a medium heat and cook, stirring continuously, for about 5 minutes until golden.

Stuff a little marzipan into the cavity of each pear half, then carefully arrange them cut-side up in the tin.

Roll out the pastry on a lightly floured surface to the size of the tin, then place over the top of the pears and press down all around them. Bake in a preheated oven, 190°C (375°F), Gas Mark 5, for about 40 minutes until the pastry is golden and the juices are bubbling. Cool in the tin for 10 minutes, then invert onto a large plate and serve hot, with ice cream or cream.

# Prune & Custard Tart

Serves 8
Preparation time 30 minutes,
 plus standing and chilling
Cooking time 45–50 minutes

4 tablespoons brandy
250 g (8 oz) ready-to-eat
 pitted prunes
150 ml (¼ pint) double cream
150 ml (¼ pint) milk
1 vanilla pod, slit in half
 lengthways
1 quantity pâte sucrée (see
 page 7), chilled
4 eggs
50 g (2 oz) caster sugar
sifted icing sugar, for dusting

Warm the brandy in a saucepan, add the prunes, simmer gently for 3–4 minutes, then take off the heat. Pour the cream and milk into a second saucepan, add the vanilla pod and bring just to the boil, then take off the heat. Cover both pans and set aside for 2 hours.

Meanwhile, roll the pastry out on a lightly floured surface to fit a buttered 24 cm (9½ inch) fluted loose-bottomed tart tin , then press the pastry over the base and sides (see page 6). Trim off the excess pastry with scissors so that it stands a little above the top of the tin. Prick the base with a fork and chill for 15 minutes.

Put the tart on a baking sheet and bake blind (see page 7) in a preheated oven, 190°C (375°F), Gas Mark 5, for 10 minutes. Remove the paper and baking beans and bake for a further 5 minutes. Remove from the oven and reduce the oven temperature to 180°C (350°F), Gas Mark 4.

Whisk the eggs and sugar together in a large bowl until creamy. Retrieve the vanilla pod, scrape out the seeds and add the seeds to the eggs, then whisk in the milk mixture.

Drain the prunes, adding excess brandy to the milk mix, then arrange in the base of the tart case. Pour over the custard and bake for 25–30 minutes until the custard is pale golden and just set. Leave to cool, then remove from the tin and dust with icing sugar to serve.

# Summer Berry Tarts

Makes 12
Preparation time 30 minutes,
   plus chilling
Cooking time 12 minutes

1 quantity pâte sucrée (see
   page 7), chilled
300 ml (½ pint) double cream
4 tablespoons lemon curd
3 tablespoons redcurrant jelly
juice of ½ lemon
250 g (8 oz) small
   strawberries, halved or
   sliced depending on size
200 g (7 oz) raspberries
150 g (5 oz) blueberries

Roll the pastry out thinly on a lightly floured surface, then stamp out 12 × 10 cm (4 inch) circles with a fluted biscuit cutter and press into a buttered 12-section muffin tin. Reknead and reroll the pastry trimmings as needed. Prick the bases 2–3 times with a fork, then chill for 15 minutes.

Line the tarts with small squares of nonstick baking paper and baking beans and bake in a preheated oven, 190°C (375°F), Gas Mark 5, for 8 minutes. Remove the paper and beans and cook for a further 4–5 minutes until golden. Leave to cool for 10 minutes, then loosen the edges and transfer to a wire rack to cool completely.

Whip the cream until it forms soft swirls, then fold in the lemon curd. Spoon into the tart cases and spread into an even layer with the back of a teaspoon.

Warm the redcurrant jelly and lemon juice together in a small saucepan, stirring, until the jelly has dissolved completely. Add the fruits and toss together. Spoon over the tarts, piling the fruit up high, then transfer to a serving plate.

# Celebration Time

Sherry Trifle
Strawberry Macaroon Cake
Black Forest Gâteau
Warm Summer Fruit Trifles
Chocolate Truffle Cake
Hazelnut Meringue Stack
Crêpes Suzette
Chocolate & Raspberry Soufflés
Chocolate Baked Alaska
Chocolate & Chestnut Roulade
Profiteroles
Cherry & Cinnamon Zabaglione
Hazelnut, Pear & Apricot Roulade
Heavenly Chocolate Puddings
Coffee Chocolate Bavarois
Chocolate Filigree Torte
Last-minute Christmas Pudding

# Sherry Trifle

**Serves 6–8**
**Preparation time 30 minutes, plus chilling**

6 trifle sponges
100 ml (3½ fl oz) sweet sherry (optional)
150 g (5 oz) raspberry jam
1 tablespoon lemon juice
250 g (8 oz) raspberries
400 ml (14 fl oz) whipping cream
25 g (1 oz) toasted flaked almonds, to decorate

**Custard**
500 ml (17 fl oz) milk
2 teaspoons vanilla extract
4 egg yolks
50 g (2 oz) caster sugar
2 teaspoons cornflour

To make the custard, place the milk and vanilla extract in a saucepan and heat until just below boiling point. Place the egg yolks, sugar and cornflour in a heatproof bowl and beat with a hand-held electric whisk until pale and thick, then gradually whisk in the warm milk. Return to the pan and cook over a medium heat for 2–3 minutes, whisking continuously, until the custard has thickened. Transfer to a bowl, cover with clingfilm to prevent a skin forming and chill.

Meanwhile, arrange the trifle sponges in the base of a 20 cm (8 inch) trifle bowl and pour over the sherry, if using. Mix together the jam and lemon juice in a bowl and spoon over the sponges. Add the raspberries and top with the cooled custard.

Lightly whip the cream in a bowl with a hand-held electric whisk until it forms soft peaks. Spoon on top of the custard and decorate with the almonds. Serve immediately or chill until ready to serve.

# Strawberry Macaroon Cake

❧❧❧

**Serves 8**
**Preparation time 40 minutes**
**Cooking time 35–45 minutes**

4 egg whites
¼ teaspoon cream of tartar
125 g (4 oz) light muscovado
   sugar
100 g (3½ oz) caster sugar
1 teaspoon white wine
   vinegar
50 g (2 oz) walnut pieces,
   lightly toasted and
   chopped

**Filling**
200 ml (7 fl oz) double cream
250 g (8 oz) strawberries

Whisk the egg whites and cream of tartar in a large clean bowl until stiff. Combine the sugars then gradually whisk into the egg white, a little at a time, until it has all been added. Whisk for a few minutes more until the meringue mixture is thick and glossy (see page 9). Fold in the walnuts.

Divide the meringue mixture evenly between 2 greased 20 cm (8 inch) sandwich tins, base-lined with nonstick baking paper. Spread the surfaces level then swirl the tops with the back of a spoon. Bake in a preheated oven, 150°C (300°F), Gas Mark 2, for 35–45 minutes until lightly browned and crisp. Loosen the edges and leave to cool in the tins.

Re-loosen the edges of the meringues and turn out on to 2 clean tea towels. Peel off the lining paper then put one of the meringues on a serving plate.

Whip the cream until softly peaking then spoon three-quarters over the meringue. Halve 8 of the smallest strawberries and set aside. Hull and slice the rest and arrange on the cream. Cover with the second meringue, top uppermost. Decorate with spoonfuls of the remaining cream and the reserved halved strawberries. Serve within 2 hours of assembly.

# Black Forest Gâteau

Serves 6
Preparation time 1 hour,
  plus cooling
Cooking time 40–45 minutes

3 large eggs
75 g (3 oz) caster sugar
50 g (2 oz) plain flour
1 tablespoon cocoa powder
1 tablespoon vegetable oil

**To finish**
425 g (14 oz) can pitted black
  cherries
1 tablespoon arrowroot
3 tablespoons kirsch
300 ml (½ pint) double cream,
  whipped
chocolate curls (see page 8)

Place the eggs and sugar into a heatproof bowl and set over a pan of gently simmering water. Whisk until thick and mousse-like. Remove the bowl from the heat, sift in the flour and cocoa powder and carefully fold into the egg mixture. Fold in the oil.

Pour the mixture in to a lined and greased 20 cm (8 inch) round cake tin and bake in a preheated oven, 190°C (375°F), Gas Mark 5, for 30–35 minutes. Remove from the oven and cool on a wire rack.

Drain the cherries and mix a little of the juice with the arrowroot in a small bowl. Pour the remaining juice into a small saucepan and bring to the boil. Pour onto the arrowroot and stir well. Return to the saucepan and heat gently, stirring, until thick and clear. Remove from the heat, add the cherries and set aside to cool.

Slice the cake in half horizontally and sprinkle both layers with kirsch. Place one layer on a serving plate and pipe a line of cream all the way around the top edge. Spread the cherry mixture in the centre and carefully top with the other layer of cake.

Spread half of the remaining cream around the sides of the gâteau and press chocolate curls into the cream to cover. Pipe the remaining cream on top of the gâteau.

# Warm Summer Fruit Trifles

**Makes 6**
**Preparation time 20 minutes**
**Cooking time 20 minutes**

8 sponge fingers or 100 g
    (3½ oz) plain sponge or
    jam-filled Swiss roll
3 tablespoons orange juice
375 g (12 oz) frozen mixed
    summer fruits, just thawed
425 g (14 oz) ready-made
    custard

**Meringue topping**
3 egg whites
75 g (3 oz) granulated sugar

Crumble the sponge fingers or cake into the bottom of
6 individual ovenproof dishes. Drizzle with the orange
juice, then add the fruits. Dollop the custard over the tops.

Whisk the egg whites in a clean, dry bowl until stiff peaks
form, then gradually whisk in the sugar, a spoonful at a
time, until all the sugar has been added. Keep whisking for
another 1–2 minutes until the mixture is thick and glossy
(see page 9).

Spoon the meringue mixture over the top of the custard in
large swirls. Place the dishes on a baking sheet. Cook in a
preheated oven, 160°C (325°F), Gas Mark 3, for 20 minutes
until the meringue is golden brown on top. Serve warm.

# Chocolate Truffle Cake

Serves 8
Preparation time 15 minutes
Cooking time 40 minutes

250 g (8 oz) plain dark
  chocolate, broken into
  pieces
125 g (4 oz) unsalted butter
50 ml (2 fl oz) double cream
4 eggs, separated
125 g (4 oz) caster sugar
2 tablespoons cocoa powder,
  sifted

Melt the chocolate, butter and cream together in a heat-proof bowl set over a saucepan of gently simmering water (see page 8). Remove from the heat and leave to cool for 5 minutes.

Whisk the egg yolks with 75 g (3 oz) of the sugar until pale and stir in the cooled chocolate mixture.

Whisk the egg whites in a large clean bowl until softly peaking then whisk in the remaining sugar. Fold into the egg yolk mixture with the sifted cocoa powder until evenly incorporated.

Pour the cake mixture into an oiled and base-lined 23 cm (9 inch) spring-form cake tin that has been lightly dusted all over with a little extra cocoa powder. Bake in a preheated oven, 180°C (350°F), Gas Mark 4, for 35 minutes.

Leave to cool in the tin for 10 minutes then turn out on to a serving plate. Serve in wedges, while still warm, with whipped cream and strawberries.

# Hazelnut Meringue Stack

❧❧❧❧❧❧

**Serves 8**
**Preparation time 10 minutes,**
  **plus cooling**
**Cooking time 45 minutes**

4 egg whites
250 g (8 oz) caster sugar
1 teaspoon white wine
  vinegar
100 g (3½ oz) blanched
  hazelnuts, toasted and
  roughly chopped
200 ml (7 fl oz) double cream
275 g (9 oz) raspberries
cocoa powder, for dusting

Line 3 baking sheets with nonstick baking paper.

Whisk the egg whites in a large clean bowl until they form stiff peaks (see page 9). Add the sugar a spoonful at a time and continue to whisk until thick and glossy. Fold in the vinegar with a large metal spoon.

Fold half the hazelnuts into the mixture, then divide it between the prepared sheets, spooning the meringue into 3 rounds roughly 18 cm (7 inches) in diameter.

Place in a preheated oven, 150°C (300°F), Gas Mark 2, for 45 minutes, then switch off the oven and leave the meringue to cool.

Whip the cream in a bowl until it forms soft peaks, spoon the cream over 2 of the meringues and top each with the raspberries and remaining nuts, reserving a few raspberries for decoration.

Stack the meringues with the plain one on top, then dust with a little cocoa powder and decorate with the remaining raspberries. Serve on the same day or chill for up to 2 days.

# Crêpes Suzette

Serves 4
Preparation time 10 minutes
Cooking time 30 minutes

125 g (4 oz) plain flour
pinch of salt
1 egg, lightly beaten
300 ml (½ pint) milk
vegetable oil or butter, for
    greasing the pan

## Orange sauce
50 g (2 oz) butter
50 g (2 oz) caster sugar
grated rind and juice of
    2 oranges
2 tablespoons Grand Marnier
2 tablespoons brandy

To make the pancakes, put the flour and salt into a bowl and make a well in the centre. Pour the egg and a little of the milk into the well. Whisk the liquid, gradually incorporating the flour to make a smooth paste. Whisk in the remaining milk, then pour the batter into a jug.

Put a little oil or butter into an 18 cm (7 inch) pancake pan or heavy-based frying pan and heat until it starts to smoke. Pour off the excess oil and pour a little batter into the pan, tilting the pan until the base is coated in a thin layer of batter. Cook the pancake for 1–2 minutes until the underside is turning golden.

Flip the pancake with a palette knife and cook for a further 30–40 seconds until it is golden on the second side. Slide the pancake out of the pancake. Make the rest of the pancakes, oiling the pan as necessary. This quantity of batter will make 8–10 pancakes. Stack the pancakes as you make them between sheets of greaseproof paper on a plate fitted over simmering water, to keep them warm while you make the rest.

To make the sauce, melt the butter in a frying pan, add the sugar, orange rind and juice and heat until bubbling. Dip each pancake into the sauce, fold it into quarters and place on a warmed serving dish. Add the Grand Marnier and brandy to the pan; heat gently and then carefully ignite. Pour the flaming liquid over the pancakes and serve immediately.

# Chocolate & Raspberry Soufflés

**Serves 4**
**Preparation time 10 minutes**
**Cooking time 13–18 minutes**

100 g (3½ oz) plain dark
    chocolate, broken into
    pieces
3 eggs, separated
50 g (2 oz) self-raising flour,
    sifted
40 g (1½ oz) caster sugar
150 g (5 oz) raspberries
icing sugar, sifted, to
    decorate

Put the chocolate in a large heatproof bowl over a saucepan of simmering water (see page 8). Leave until melted, then remove from the heat and allow to cool a little. Whisk in the egg yolks and fold in the flour.

Whisk the egg whites and caster sugar in a medium bowl until they form soft peaks. Beat a spoonful of the egg whites into the chocolate mixture to loosen it before gently folding in the rest.

Put the raspberries into 4 lightly greased ramekins, pour over the chocolate mixture and cook in a preheated oven, 190°C (375°F), Gas Mark 5, for 12–15 minutes until the soufflés have risen.

# Chocolate Baked Alaska

❧❧❧

**Serves 4–6**
**Preparation time 10 minutes,**
**plus freezing**
**Cooking time 5 minutes**

1 small sponge flan case
2 tablespoons apple juice or
  chocolate liqueur
4 tablespoons cherry,
  raspberry or strawberry jam
500 ml (17 fl oz) tall tub luxury
  chocolate ice cream
3 egg whites
125 g (4 oz) golden caster
  sugar

Place the sponge flan case in an ovenproof pie dish. Drizzle over the apple juice or chocolate liqueur, then spoon on the jam and spread it over evenly.

Run a blunt knife around the sides of the ice cream to help loosen it from the tub. Upturn the ice cream on top of the sponge flan case. Place on a flat surface in the freezer.

Whisk the egg whites in a grease-free bowl until thick. Gradually whisk in the sugar until the meringue is thick and glossy (see page 9).

Spread the meringue over the prepared ice cream base using a palette knife, making sure the ice cream is completely covered and the meringue seals the edge of the sponge flan case. Return to the freezer for at least 1 hour (you can leave it for up to a day).

Bake in a preheated oven, 220°C (425°F), Gas Mark 7, for 5 minutes until the meringue is just starting to get tinged with brown, then serve immediately.

# Chocolate & Chestnut Roulade

Serves 8
Preparation time 15 minutes
Cooking time 20 minutes

6 eggs, separated
125 g (4 oz) caster sugar
2 tablespoons cocoa powder
icing sugar, for dusting

**Filling**
150 ml (¼ pint) double cream
100 g (3½ oz) chestnut purée
  or sweetened chestnut
  spread

Grease and line a 29 x 18 cm (11½ x 7 inch) Swiss roll tin. Whisk the egg whites in a large clean bowl until they form soft peaks. Whisk together the egg yolks and sugar in a separate bowl until thick and pale. Fold the cocoa powder and egg whites into the egg yolk mixture.

Spoon the mixture into the prepared tin and place in a preheated oven, 180°C (350°F), Gas Mark 4, for 20 minutes. Remove from the oven and cool in the tin.

Turn the cooled sponge out on to a piece of greaseproof paper dusted with icing sugar.

Whip the cream for the filling in a large clean bowl until it forms soft peaks. Fold the chestnut purée or sweetened chestnut spread into the cream, then smooth the filling over the sponge.

Using the greaseproof paper to help you, carefully roll up the roulade from one short end and lift it gently on to its serving dish. (Don't worry if it cracks: it won't detract from its appearance or taste.) Dust with icing sugar. Chill until needed and eat on the day it is made.

# Profiteroles

Serves 6
Preparation time 40 minutes,
 plus cooling
Cooking time 35–40 minutes

50 g (2 oz) unsalted butter
150 ml (¼ pint) water
65 g (2½ oz) plain flour, sifted
2 eggs, beaten

## Filling
1 tablespoon icing sugar,
 sifted
2–3 drops vanilla extract
175 ml (6 fl oz) double cream,
 whipped

## To serve
1 quantity easy peasy
 chocolate sauce (see page
 186)

Melt the butter in a large heavy-based saucepan, add the measurement water and bring to the boil. Remove the pan from the heat, add the flour all at once and beat until the mixture leaves the sides of the saucepan. Cool slightly, then add the eggs a little at a time, beating vigorously.

Put the mixture into a piping bag fitted with a plain 1 cm (½ inch) nozzle, and pipe small mounds of mixture on a dampened baking sheet.

Bake in a preheated oven, 220°C (425°F), Gas Mark 7, for 10 minutes, then lower the temperature to 190°C (375°F), Gas Mark 5, and bake for a further 20–25 minutes until golden. Remove from the heat, make a slit in the side of each bun and cool on wire rack.

To make the filling, fold the icing sugar and vanilla extract into the cream. Pipe or spoon a little into each profiterole. Pile the profiteroles on a serving dish.

Make the chocolate sauce (see page 186), pour over the profiteroles and serve.

# Cherry & Cinnamon Zabaglione

**Serves 4**
**Preparation time 10 minutes**
**Cooking time 10–15 minutes**

4 egg yolks
125 g (4 oz) caster sugar
150 ml (¼ pint) cream sherry
large pinch of ground
   cinnamon, plus extra to
   decorate
400 g (13 oz) can pitted black
   cherries in syrup

Pour 5 cm (2 inches) water into a medium pan and bring to the boil. Set a large heatproof bowl over the pan, making sure that the water does not touch the base of the bowl. Reduce the heat so that the water is simmering, then add the egg yolks, sugar, sherry and cinnamon to the bowl. Whisk for 5–8 minutes or until very thick and foamy and the custard leaves a trail when the whisk is lifted above the mixture.

Drain off some of the cherry syrup and then tip the cherries and just a little of the syrup into a small saucepan. Warm through, then spoon into 4 glasses. Pour the warm zabaglione over the top and serve dusted with cinnamon and with amaretti biscuits.

# Hazelnut, Pear & Apricot Roulade

**Serves 6–8**
**Preparation time 30 minutes, plus cooling**
**Cooking time 18–20 minutes**

125 g (4 oz) hazelnuts
5 eggs, separated
175 g (6 oz) caster sugar, plus extra for sprinkling
1 just-ripe pear, peeled and coarsely grated
200 g (7 oz) mascarpone cheese
2 tablespoons icing sugar
250 g (8 oz) fresh apricots, roughly chopped

Grease and line a 30 x 23 cm (12 x 9 inch) roasting tin with nonstick baking paper, snipping diagonally into the corners so it lines the base and sides. Place the nuts on a piece of foil and toast under the grill for 3–4 minutes until golden. Roughly chop 2 tablespoons and reserve for decoration, then finely chop the remainder.

Whisk the yolks and sugar until they are thick and pale and the whisk leaves a trail. Fold in the finely chopped hazelnuts and pear. Whisk the whites into stiff, moist-looking peaks. Fold a large spoonful into the nut mix to loosen it, then gently fold in the remaining egg whites.

Spoon the mixture into the prepared tin. Bake the roulade in a preheated oven, 180°C (350°F), Gas Mark 4, for 15 minutes until golden brown and the top feels spongy. Cover and leave to cool for at least 1 hour.

Beat the mascarpone and icing sugar together until soft. On a work surface, cover a damp tea towel with baking paper and sprinkle with sugar. Turn the roulade on to the paper and remove the tin and lining paper.

Spread the roulade with the mascarpone mixture, then with the apricots. Roll up the roulade, starting from the short end nearest you, using the paper and tea towel to help. Transfer the roulade to a serving plate, sprinkle over the reserved hazelnuts and cut into thick slices.

# Heavenly Chocolate Puddings

**Serves 4**
**Preparation time 10 minutes**
**Cooking time 10 minutes**

100 g (3½ oz) milk chocolate, broken up
50 g (2 oz) unsalted butter
40 g (1½ oz) cocoa powder
75 g (3 oz) golden caster sugar
2 eggs, separated
1 teaspoon vanilla extract
4 tablespoons single cream
icing sugar, for dusting

Melt the chocolate and butter in a large mixing bowl placed over a pan of barely simmering water (see page 8), making sure the surface of the water does not touch the bowl. Remove from the heat, add the cocoa powder, 50 g (2 oz) of the sugar, the egg yolks, vanilla extract and cream and beat the mixture to a smooth paste.

Whisk the egg whites in a clean bowl until peaking and gradually whisk in the remaining sugar. Use a large metal spoon to fold a quarter of the meringue into the chocolate mixture to lighten it, then fold in the remainder.

Spoon the mixture into 4 small ramekin dishes or similar-sized ovenproof dishes. Bake in a preheated oven, 160°C (325°F), Gas Mark 3, for 8–10 minutes or until a very thin crust has formed over the surface. Dust with icing sugar and serve immediately.

# Coffee Chocolate Bavarois

Serves 10
Preparation time 45 minutes,
    plus freezing and chilling
Cooking time 10 minutes

1 litre (1¾ pints) single cream
150 g (5 oz) plain dark
    chocolate, chopped
2 teaspoons cornflour
150 g (5 oz) golden caster
    sugar
8 egg yolks
25 g (1 oz) powdered gelatine
1 tablespoon fresh espresso
    coffee, extremely strong
4 tablespoons coffee liqueur

Line a 1 kg (2 lb) loaf tin with nonstick baking paper and place in the freezer to chill.

Heat half the cream gently in a pan. Add the chocolate and stir until melted. Remove from the heat.

Put half the cornflour, half the sugar and 4 egg yolks in a bowl. Put the remaining cornflour, sugar and yolks in a second bowl. Stir, then slowly whisk the chocolate cream into one bowl. Return to the pan and heat gently, stirring until slightly thickened and smooth. Whisk in half the powdered gelatine, then pour into a jug.

Pour half the chocolate cream into the base of the prepared loaf tin. Freeze uncovered, on a flat surface, for 45 minutes until just set.

Combine the remaining cream, espresso coffee and coffee liqueur in a pan over a low heat. Whisk this into the mixture in the second bowl, transfer to the pan and warm through. Add the rest of the gelatine and whisk together. Remove from the heat and pour into a jug.

Pour half the coffee cream over the set chocolate cream and refreeze for another 30 minutes or until just set. Pour over the remaining chocolate cream and freeze for 20 minutes, until just set, then pour on the final coffee cream layer. Chill for 4 hours. Run a knife around the sides, turn on to a board and slice to serve.

# Chocolate Filigree Torte

Serves 10
Preparation time 30 minutes,
  plus cooling and chilling
Cooking time 20–25 minutes

3 eggs
75 g (3 oz) caster sugar
50 g (2 oz) plain flour
25 g (1 oz) cocoa powder

**Filling**
2 teaspoons powdered
  gelatine
3 tablespoons cold water
200 g (7 oz) plain dark
  chocolate
500 g (1 lb) mascarpone
  cheese, at room
  temperature
75 g (3 oz) caster sugar
1 teaspoon vanilla extract
200 g (7 oz) Greek yogurt
4 tablespoons hot water

Whisk the eggs and sugar in a bowl over a pan of hot water until thickened. Remove from the heat and whisk for 2 minutes. Sift over the flour and cocoa powder, then fold in. Turn into a greased and lined 23 cm (9 inch) springform or loose-based cake tin.

Bake in a preheated oven, 190°C (375°F), Gas Mark 5, for 15 minutes until just firm. Cool on a wire rack.

Sprinkle the gelatine over the measurement cold water in a bowl and leave for 5 minutes. Split the sponge and put one half in the cake tin. Stand the bowl of gelatine in a pan of hot water until the gelatine has melted.

Melt 175 g (6 oz) chocolate over a pan of simmering water (see page 8). Beat the mascarpone in a bowl with the sugar, vanilla extract, yogurt and measurement hot water. Whisking well, gradually pour the gelatine mix into the mascarpone mix. Spoon half into a separate bowl and beat in the chocolate. Turn the chocolate mix into the tin. Cover with the second sponge, then the remaining mascarpone (if this has started to set, beat in a little hot water). Level the surface and chill for several hours.

Transfer to a serving plate. Remove the greaseproof paper. Melt the remaining chocolate and drizzle it over the top. Chill until ready to serve.

# Last-minute Christmas Pudding

❧❧❧ ❧❧❧ ❧❧❧

**Serves 8**
**Preparation time 30 minutes,**
**plus standing**
**Cooking time 6–7 hours**

125 g (4 oz) dark molasses
 sugar
200 g (7 oz) fresh white
 breadcrumbs
125 g (4 oz) shredded suet
pinch of salt
1 teaspoon ground mixed
 spice
175 g (6 oz) sultanas
175 g (6 oz) pitted raisins
125 g (4 oz) currants
50 g (2 oz) candied peel,
 chopped
25 g (1 oz) blanched almonds,
 finely chopped
1 large cooking apple,
 peeled, cored and finely
 chopped
finely grated rind and juice of
 ½ lemon
1 egg, beaten
150 ml (¼ pint) Guinness or
 milk stout
about 75 ml (3 fl oz) milk
icing sugar, for dusting
2 tablespoons brandy, to serve

Put the dry ingredients, dried fruit, candied peel and almonds into a large bowl and stir well to mix. Add the apple with the lemon rind and juice, egg and Guinness or milk stout and stir well. Add enough milk to make a soft dropping consistency.

Turn into a greased 1.2 litre (2 pint) pudding basin. Cover the top of the pudding with a circle of greased greaseproof paper, then with foil, or tie up the basin in a pudding cloth. Fold a pleat in the centre and tie string around the rim. Leave to stand overnight.

Place the basin in the top of a steamer or double boiler, or in a large pan of gently bubbling water, and steam for 4–5 hours, topping up with more boiling water as necessary.

Remove the basin carefully from the pan and leave to cool completely. Discard the foil and greaseproof paper. Replace with fresh greaseproof paper and foil if you intend to store the pudding, but it doesn't need to mature and can be made just before Christmas.

Steam again for 2 hours before serving. Dust with icing sugar and decorate with a holly leaf, if liked. Warm the brandy, pour over the pudding and set alight. Serve with cream or brandy butter, rum butter or brandy cream.

# Really Easy

Chocolate & Raspberry Pudding
Elderflower Poached Pears
Mixed Berry Salad
Port & Cherry Compote
Raspberry & Honey Cranachan
Quick Tiramisu
Spiced Oven-roasted Plums
Cider Syllabub
Apple Snow
Cherry Clafoutis
Instant Apple Crumbles
Freeform Apple Tart
Baked Pears with Marzipan
Winter Dried Fruit Salad
Easy Peasy Chocolate Sauce
Sabayon

# Chocolate & Raspberry Pudding

**Serves 6**
**Preparation time 15 minutes**
**Cooking time 40–45 minutes**

175 g (6 oz) fresh raspberries
125 g (4 oz) self-raising flour
40 g (1½ oz) cocoa powder
100 g (3½ oz) caster sugar
250 ml (8 fl oz) milk
75 g (3 oz) unsalted butter,
  melted
2 eggs, beaten

### Topping
75 g (3 oz) caster sugar
75 g (3 oz) soft light brown
  sugar
2 tablespoons cocoa powder
350 ml (12 fl oz) boiling water
icing sugar, for dusting

Lighty grease a 1 litre (1¾ pint) baking dish. Scatter the raspberries over the base of the dish.

Sift the flour and cocoa powder into a bowl and stir in the caster sugar. Make a well in the centre and whisk in the milk, melted butter and eggs to form a smooth batter (it should be quite runny). Pour the mixture into the dish, covering the raspberries.

Make the topping. Combine the sugars and cocoa powder and sprinkle over the top of the chocolate mixture. Very carefully pour the measurement boiling water over the top as evenly as possible.

Bake in a preheated oven, 180°C (350°F), Gas Mark 4, for 40–45 minutes until the pudding is firm to the touch and some 'bubbles' of sauce appear on the top. Rest for 5 minutes, then dust with icing sugar and serve.

# Elderflower Poached Pears

Serves 4
Preparation time 5 minutes,
    plus cooling
Cooking time 25 minutes

125 ml (4 fl oz) elderflower
    and pear or elderflower and
    apple cordial
500 ml (17 fl oz) apple juice
2 teaspoons lemon juice
4 large pears, peeled, cored
    and quartered
pinch of saffron threads

Mix the cordial, apple juice and lemon juice in a small, deep saucepan. Bring to a gentle simmer and add the pears and saffron. Simmer gently for about 25 minutes or until the pears are tender.

Remove from the heat, cover and leave to cool completely in the poaching liquid. Carefully remove the pears with a slotted spoon and divide into serving bowls. Ladle over the poaching liquid to serve.

# Mixed Berry Salad

**Serves 4–6**
**Preparation time 10 minutes**

400 g (13 oz) strawberries
250 g (8 oz) raspberries
150 g (5 oz) blueberries
150 g (5 oz) blackberries
1 small bunch of mint, finely
   chopped, a few sprigs
   reserved for decoration
3 tablespoons elderflower
   syrup

Hull and halve the strawberries. Wash all the berries and
drain well.

Put the berries in a large serving bowl and add the chopped
mint and elderflower syrup. Mix together carefully and
serve, decorated with the reserved mint sprigs.

# Port & Cherry Compote

Serves 4
Preparation time 15 minutes,
plus cooling
Cooking time 10 minutes

750 g (1½ lb) fresh cherries,
stoned
2 tablespoons redcurrant jelly
125 ml (4 fl oz) port
thinly pared rind and juice of
1 orange
2 teaspoons arrowroot

Place the cherries in a heavy-based saucepan with the redcurrant jelly , port and orange rind. Cover and bring slowly to the boil. Stir gently and simmer for 4–5 minutes.

Take off the heat and transfer the cherries to individual serving dishes with a slotted spoon. Remove the orange rind.

Blend the orange juice with the arrowroot, then add to the cherry syrup in the saucepan. Bring to the boil, stirring and simmer for 1 minute. Remove from the heat, allow to cool and then pour over the cherries.

# Raspberry & Honey Cranachan

**Serves 4**
**Preparation time 10 minutes**

50 g (2 oz) medium oatmeal
2 tablespoons whisky
250 ml (8 fl oz) double cream
250 g (8 oz) raspberries
3 tablespoons clear honey

Place the oatmeal in a nonstick frying pan over a medium heat and dry-fry for 2–3 minutes, stirring continuously, until toasted. Transfer to a plate to cool.

Meanwhile, whip the whisky and cream with a hand-held electric whisk in a bowl until it forms soft peaks. Place a handful of the raspberries in a separate bowl and crush with a fork.

Stir the oatmeal, honey, crushed raspberries and remaining raspberries into the whisky-cream. Spoon into 4 glasses and serve immediately.

# Quick Tiramisu

Serves 4–6
Preparation time 15 minutes,
  plus chilling

5 tablespoons strong
  espresso coffee
75 g (3 oz) dark muscovado
  sugar
4 tablespoons coffee liqueur
  or 3 tablespoons brandy
75 g (3 oz) sponge finger
  biscuits, broken into large
  pieces
400 g (13 oz) good-quality
  ready-made custard
250 g (8 oz) mascarpone
  cheese
1 teaspoon vanilla extract
75 g (3 oz) plain chocolate,
  finely chopped
cocoa powder, for dusting

Mix the coffee with 2 tablespoons of the sugar and the liqueur or brandy in a medium bowl. Toss the sponge fingers in the mixture and turn into a serving dish, spooning over any excess liquid.

Beat together the custard, mascarpone and vanilla extract and spoon a third of the mixture over the biscuits. Sprinkle with the remaining sugar, then spoon over half the remaining custard. Scatter with half the chopped chocolate, then spread with the remaining custard and sprinkle with the remaining chopped chocolate.

Chill for about 1 hour until set. Serve dusted with cocoa powder.

# Spiced Oven-roasted Plums

**Serves 4**
**Preparation time 5 minutes**
**Cooking time 25–30 minutes**

8 ripe red plums
1 cinnamon stick
2 star anise
50 g (2 oz) demerara sugar
grated rind and juice of 1
    orange
2 tablespoons orange liqueur
2 tablespoons water

Place the whole plums, cinnamon stick and star anise in a shallow ovenproof dish. Scatter over the sugar, then add the orange rind and juice, orange liqueur and measurement water.

Place in a preheated oven, 200°C (400°F), Gas Mark 6, for 25–30 minutes, basting halfway through the cooking time.

Spoon the plums into bowls and pour over some of the syrup. Serve immediately.

# Cider Syllabub

**Serves 6**
**Preparation time 15 minutes**

300 ml (½ pint) double cream
grated rind and juice of
   1 lemon
125 ml (4 fl oz) sweet cider
2 egg whites
50 g (2 oz) caster sugar

Put the cream and lemon rind in a large bowl and whisk until thick. Gradually add the lemon juice and cider and continue whisking until it holds its shape.

Whisk the egg whites until stiff. Whisk in the sugar, then carefully fold in the cream mixture.

Spoon into individual serving dishes and serve with shortbread fingers.

# Apple Snow

**Serves 4**
**Preparation time 20 minutes,**
   **plus cooling**
**Cooking time 10–15 minutes**

500 g (1 lb) cooking apples,
   peeled, cored and sliced
50 g (2 oz) caster sugar
2 tablespoons water
2 egg whites
grated rind and juice of
   ½ lemon

Place the apples in a saucepan, sprinkle with the sugar and add the measurement water. Cover and simmer gently for 10–15 minutes, then place in a liquidizer or food processor and blend to a purée. Leave to cool.

Whisk the egg whites until stiff and fold into the apple purée with the lemon rind and juice.

Spoon into individual serving dishes and serve immediately with sponge fingers.

# Cherry Clafoutis

Serves 4
Preparation time 10 minutes
Cooking time 20–25 minutes

32 fresh or canned cherries,
  pitted
4 tablespoons kirsch
3 tablespoons caster sugar
25 g (1 oz) plain flour, sifted
4 eggs, beaten
100 ml (3½ fl oz) double
  cream
6 tablespoons milk
½ teaspoon vanilla extract

Grease 4 x 250 ml (8 fl oz) ramekins or ovenproof dishes
and place on a baking sheet. Divide the cherries evenly
between the dishes and spoon 1 tablespoon of the kirsch
over each.

Place the sugar, flour and eggs in a bowl and beat together
with a hand-held electric whisk until light and well blended.
Whisk in the cream, milk and vanilla extract.

Pour the batter over the top of the cherries and place the
dishes in a preheated oven, 190°C (375°F), Gas Mark 5,
for 20–25 minutes or until the batter has set. Serve
immediately.

# Instant Apple Crumbles

**Serves 4**
**Preparation time 7 minutes**
**Cooking time 13 minutes**

1 kg (2 lb) Bramley apples,
   peeled, cored and thickly
   sliced
25 g (1 oz) butter
2 tablespoons caster sugar
1 tablespoon lemon juice
2 tablespoons water

**Crumble**
50 g (2 oz) butter
75 g (3 oz) fresh wholemeal
   breadcrumbs
25 g (1 oz) pumpkin seeds
2 tablespoons soft brown
   sugar

Place the apples in a saucepan with the butter, sugar, lemon juice and measurement water. Cover and simmer for 8–10 minutes, until softened.

Melt the butter for the crumble in a frying pan, add the breadcrumbs and stir-fry until lightly golden, then add the pumpkin seeds and stir-fry for a further 1 minute. Remove from the heat and stir in the sugar.

Spoon the apple mixture into bowls, sprinkle with the crumble and serve with cream or ice cream.

# Freeform Apple Tart

**Serves 6**
**Preparation time 10 minutes**
**Cooking time 20–25 minutes**

1 large sheet of shortcrust
  pastry, 30 cm (12 inch)
  square, thawed if frozen
500 g (1 lb) Granny Smith
  apples, peeled, cored and
  thinly sliced
50 g (2 oz) raisins
25 g (1 oz) soft light brown
  sugar
25 g (1 oz) butter, melted
½ teaspoon ground cinnamon
1 tablespoon milk
1 tablespoon icing sugar, plus
  extra to serve

Lay the pastry sheet on a baking sheet lined with nonstick baking paper and trim each corner to make a roughly round piece of pastry.

Mix together the apples, raisins, brown sugar, melted butter and cinnamon in a bowl until evenly combined. Spoon the apple mixture on to the pastry sheet, arranging it in a circle, leaving a 2.5 cm (1 inch) border. Pull the pastry edges up and over the filling to make a rim. Brush the pastry with the milk and dust with the icing sugar.

Bake in a preheated oven, 180°C (350°F), Gas Mark 4, for 20–25 minutes until the pastry is golden and the fruit softened. Dust with extra icing sugar and serve warm with custard.

# Baked Pears with Marzipan

**Serves 4**
**Preparation time 10 minutes**
**Cooking time 25–30 minutes**

4 pears, peeled, keeping
   the pears whole
juice of ½ lemon
50 g (2 oz) marzipan, grated
   or finely chopped
1 tablespoon sultanas
4 tablespoons apple juice
2 tablespoons runny honey
2 tablespoons flaked
   almonds, toasted

Core the pears from the bases, leaving the stalks in place, and coat with the lemon juice. Mix together the marzipan and sultanas in a bowl, then spoon the mixture into the cored cavity of the pears. Stand the stuffed pears in a small ovenproof dish.

Spoon over the apple juice, then drizzle over the honey and place in a preheated oven, 180°C (350°F), Gas Mark 4, for 25–30 minutes until tender. Remove from the oven and scatter over the almonds. Serve with cream or custard.

# Winter Dried Fruit Salad

Serves 6
Preparation time 5 minutes,
  plus soaking
Cooking time 10–15 minutes

175 g (6 oz) dried apricots
125 g (4 oz) dried prunes
125 g (4 oz) dried figs
125 g (4 oz) dried apples
600 ml (1 pint) apple juice
2 tablespoons Calvados or
  brandy
25 g (1 oz) walnuts, roughly
  chopped

Place the dried fruits in a bowl with the apple juice and leave to soak overnight.

Transfer the fruits and juice to a saucepan and simmer for 10–15 minutes.

Turn into a glass bowl and pour over the Calvados or brandy. Sprinkle with the walnuts. Serve warm or cold with crème fraîche or cream.

# Easy Peasy Chocolate Sauce

**Serves 4**
**Preparation time 2 minutes**
**Cooking time 3 minutes**

175 g (6 oz) evaporated milk
100 g (3½ oz) plain dark
  chocolate, broken into
  pieces

Tip the evaporated milk into a pan, add the chocolate and heat gently for 2–3 minutes, stirring until the chocolate is melted.

Serve immediately with the dessert of your choice. This sauce goes particularly well with ice cream.

# Sabayon

Serves 4–6
Preparation time 5 minutes
Cooking time 5 minutes

4 egg yolks
4 tablespoons caster sugar
100 ml (3½ fl oz) dessert wine
2 tablespoons water

Put all the ingredients in a heatproof bowl. Rest the bowl over a saucepan of gently simmering water, making sure that the bowl doesn't touch the water.

Beat the mixture using a hand-held electric whisk or balloon whisk for about 5 minutes, until it is very thick and foamy – the whisk should leave a trail when it is lifted from the bowl.

Remove the bowl from the heat and whisk for a further 2 minutes. Spoon the sabayon into glasses or a warmed jug and serve immediately (it will collapse if left to stand) with thin shortbread biscuits.

# Index

# Acknowledgements

Special photography © Octopus Publishing Group Limited/Stephen Conroy 2 (bottom left), 10 (top left),16, 49, 54, 62 (top left) 65, 68, 79, 101,107, 112 (top right, bottom left, bottom right), 115, 116, 124, 127, 128, 131, 134, 137, 138 (bottom left), 145, 151,157, 161, 187; /Vanessa Davies 62 (bottom right), 85; /Will Heap 2 (top left), 6, 7, 8, 9, 10 (bottom left), 13, 14, 27, 29, 31, 33, 36 (bottom left, bottom right), 39, 40, 59, 86 (bottom right), 86 (top left) 89, 90, 98, 104, 141, 169 (bottom right), 175, 176, 178, 180, 181; /Jeremy Hopley 45; /David Munns 83, 152, 162, 186; /Emma Neish 149, 155; /Lis Parsons 18, 74, 80, 92, 100, 133, 138 (bottom right), 158, 166, 168 (top left), 173, 185; /Gareth Sambridge 95; /William Shaw 2 (top right, bottom right), 10 (top left, bottom right), 21, 22, 25, 34, 53, 57, 60, 86 (bottom left), 97, 108, 111, 120, 123, 138 (top left, top right), 143, 146, 168 (top right), 172, 184; /Ian Wallace 36 (top left, top right), 43, 46, 50, 62 (top right), 62 (bottom left), 70, 77, 86 (top right), 103, 112 (top left), 119, 165, 168 (bottom left), 171, 183.